College Courses in the High School

Franklin P. Wilbur
David W. Chapman

National Association of Secondary School Principals
Reston, Virginia

About the authors: Franklin P. Wilbur is an associate in development and David W. Chapman is an associate in research and evaluation at the Center for Instructional Development, Syracuse University, Syracuse, N.Y. Dr. Chapman is also a member of Research, Evaluation & Design Associates, 2650 Lakeview Drive, Chicago, Ill., and Dr. Wilbur is affiliated with Development and Evaluation Associates, Room 606 Midtown Plaza, 600 Water Street, Syracuse, N.Y.

ISBN 0-88210-089-0

Contents

Foreword   vii

Introduction   ix

1. High School-College Cooperative Programs: 1
   Rationale and Overview

2. Establishing and Maintaining Cooperative   12
   Programs

3. The Role of Evaluation Within a Cooperative   44
   Program

4. Questions You Should Ask Any College or   63
   University Wanting To Work with Your School

5. Summary and Conclusions   70

Appendix
   Directory of schools cooperatively sponsoring
      programs with colleges and universities   75
   Sample credit transfer survey instruments   79
   Examples of questions used on the Project Advance   84
   Course Evaluation (PACE) form

References   87

Selected Bibliography   91

List of Tables and Figures

Tables

1 Four General Models of School-College   9
  Curriculum Articulation Arrangements

2 Budget Categories To Be Considered in   18
  Determining the Financial Structure of a
  School-College Cooperative Program

3 Primary Audiences of Evaluation of High   45
  School-College Cooperative Programs

4 Example of Judges' Description of Project   52
  Advance and Syracuse University Papers Written
  at Level II

5 Sample Chart for Comparing Features of Two or   66
  More School-College Cooperative Programs

Figures

1 Process Model for Instructional Development   23

2 Approximate Timeline and Activities Preceding   27
  the Implementation of Syracuse University
  Project Advance

3 Miniquest   58

Acknowledgements

We wish to thank our colleague and good friend, Mr. Joseph W. Lafay, Jr., for the many hours he spent editing the manuscript and for his encouragement throughout the writing period. We would also like to thank Ms. Bette Gaines for reading and commenting on selected chapters; and, to the entire Project Advance staff, we would like to express our appreciation for their support, especially to Ms. Debra Purtell, who did all the preliminary typing. And finally, thank the high school and university administrators and faculty throughout the Project Advance network whose cooperation has helped make SUPA a success.

Foreword

Finding ways to expand learning opportunities for youth is a central aim of NASSP. For almost a decade your Association has sponsored publications and conferences in support of action learning, providing students a learning environment in off-campus settings as well as in the classroom. Schools were alert to the times, resulting in the rapid growth of work experience and community service programs, of career internships, and of apprenticeships.

The range of community resources should be viewed vertically as well as horizontally. Not only should students have the opportunity to learn outward beyond the classroom, they also should have expanded opportunities to learn upward toward higher education. In today's world students are ready for this step with support from their parents and the general citizenry.

A number of forces are converging to make it so: a more serious student, the push to recapture better test scores, the demand for accountability, the focus on outcomes rather than inputs, the total cost of schooling, and a consumer-oriented society with its emphasis on accessibility for the customer.

Teaching college courses in high schools to high school students is an idea whose time has come. Already implemented successfully in approximately 100 institutions, the program promises important dividends to participating students. As was pointed out in NASSP's *This We Believe*, this approach not only provides students with a new challenge to offset the senior doldrums, it also gives students the opportunity to try their hand at the rigors of college course work while still in a familiar and supportive setting. It provides, in fact, the ideal transition ladder from high school to higher education—a ladder in the past with too many missing rungs.

This monograph gives the background of school-college cooperative programs, documenting past efforts as well as present needs. It then outlines specific steps that may be taken to plan, develop, and evaluate these programs.

The authors, richly experienced, have written a practical yet far-reaching document. We urge you to consider its immediate advantage for students as well as its long-range implications. College-bound seniors are seeking new challenges and they will find those challenges either as a part of their high school program or elsewhere.

Accessibility and quality are the watchwords in education today. A strong school-college cooperative program provides for both without adding significant costs.

Owen B. Kiernan
Executive Director
NASSP

Introduction

As a secondary school principal, I have found it especially discouraging to see many capable high school seniors lose interest in school. Senioritis, as this combination of boredom and restlessness has been called, is not new, but it seems to have grown dramatically in the 1970s. High school seniors who have completed most of their graduation requirements by the end of their junior year frequently idle away the last year of school, and thus waste time and lose some of the keenness for hard study that they will need for college work.

One traditional response to this problem has itself created difficulties: as the high school curriculum is enriched by offering more advanced subjects, the likelihood of course duplication in the freshman year of college is also increased. Returning students have complained that their first college courses have simply repeated material they had already learned in high school.

We at Manhasset wanted to respond to increasing student requests for early graduation, but we believed that an imaginative high school program could provide the kinds of experiences students were seeking through early graduation. We decided to investigate the possibility of college programs that could be taught during the senior year of high school and taught as part of the "regular" curriculum.

As college programs available in our region were discussed, members of our guidance staff and department chairpersons reviewed the curriculum and procedural aspects of each possibility carefully. Many questions had to be answered. Was the college anxious to bridge the gap between grades 12 and 13, or was it chiefly interested in attracting more students to its campus during the declining enrollment period of the '80s? Were the courses identical to those taught on the college campus? Would there be adequate training programs or workshop sessions for staff to discuss course content and standards freely? What kind of rapport could our staff expect from their college counterparts?

Our guidance counselors also contributed important questions to the discussion that would be asked by students and parents who, up to this point, had been accustomed only to the Advanced Placement courses. To be sure, we had no intention of eliminating the successful aspects of the Advanced Placement program. We also wanted to make certain that any course offered for college credit would prepare the students to take the Advanced Placement examination should they choose that route.

Moreover, we were interested in finding a program that admitted *motivated* students. Much of our concern centered on the A- and B+ students who did not qualify for programs for the gifted and talented but who had completed their high school requirements by the end of their junior year and were motivated to move on to the next academic level.

After considerable investigation, we adopted Syracuse University's Project Advance. Starting slowly, we worked with the freshman college English course during our first and second years. Staff, student, and parent reaction were all excellent. Graduates of the program reported very positive results, not the least of which was their ability to tackle the tremendous writing requirements of college courses with relative ease.

Midway in our second year with Project Advance, we decided to add calculus, biology, psychology, and sociology courses. Our students have met with equal success in these areas.

Staff members now feel that we have taken a giant step toward eliminating curricular discontinuity between our senior year and the first year of college. In addition, our own curriculum development has benefited. All faculty members in each department are now fully aware of the demands placed on students at the next level of instruction. This perspective has helped to focus our curriculum improvement projects. Some might call this curriculum development from the top. To us the important factor is that new stimulation and improvement are taking place with our curriculum.

Another positive feature of our cooperative program is the exchange of ideas and materials that has occurred between the secondary school and university staff members. These contacts have been continuous and most healthy for all. Suggestions from the Manhasset faculty for course improvement have been weighed carefully by university staff and frequently are incorporated into the program.

Student response has been very positive. For students in the program—in our case approximately one-third of the senior class—the advantage of moving ahead with their liberal arts requirements and of learning to deal with the rigors of college course work is paramount. It develops confidence as well as new skills. Waiver of requirements upon arrival at college, advanced standing, and, in many cases, credit toward the bachelor's degree are additional benefits. Few students, indeed, have used these credits to shorten their college program. Rather, they tend to substitute courses in their fields of major interest. The few students who do shorten their bachelor's degree program are anticipating earlier entrance to graduate school.

High school-college cooperative programs are not without their problems, however. The major problem, in my opinion, has to do with transferability of credit to other colleges. Seniors who succeed in college-level subjects want tangible recognition of their achievement in the form of *transfer* credit. In short, they want their credit to be accepted by the college of their choice. College catalogs and admissions officers are much too vague in this regard. Students in the junior year, planning one or more college courses for their senior year, should be thoroughly briefed concerning the acceptance of their college credit.

While transfer credit is generally granted, it is not consistently granted, we have found. Colleges and universities have, of course, a right to withhold transfer credit if they are not satisfied that the credit represents respectable college achievement, but some institutions seem to have an unreasoning prejudice against college credit earned off campus simply because it has been earned off campus. Colleges have an obligation to state in their catalogs, very clearly, the procedure students must follow to have transfer credit accepted for college-level work taken in high school. Currently the American Council of Education, in cooperation with the American Association of Collegiate Registrars and Admissions Officers and the Council on Post-Secondary Education, has formed a joint task force to study the problem of transfer of credit at the college level.

The program of college courses we have adopted works well for our student population. Perhaps all secondary school administrators should consider new steps to increase the opportunities available to their students for college-level work as well as initiate improved school-college articulation in the curriculum. If they should do so, their preliminary work will be considerably reduced by the present monograph. *College Courses in the High School* explains high school-college cooperative programs: how they originated, how they can be established or joined, how they are regulated and supervised, in short, most of the things that high school administrators would want to know about this educational innovation. Moreover, the monograph is not simply one more theoretical discussion of articulation programs, valuable as these may be. It has evolved principally out of the authors' practical experience with one of the most successful and carefully thought out cooperative programs in the country.

> Warren M. McGregor, Principal
> Manhasset Junior-Senior High School
> Manhasset, New York

1. High School-College Cooperative Programs

School-university cooperation is typical of educational sacred cows. Everyone favors it, few practice it, and hardly anyone realistically describes the result. . . . Many, if not most, cooperative ventures experience tension, frustration, and ultimate failure.

—Alan Tom

IN RECENT YEARS there has been interest in high school-college cooperative programs, but, as Alan Tom's quotation indicates, there has been more interest than practice, and more practice than success. This monograph has been written to assist high school administrators translate their interest in articulation programs into actual practice and to ensure, as far as possible, that their efforts succeed.

While the potential benefits are great, the difficulty of nurturing school-college programs should not be underestimated. Principals are not likely to be surprised, however, by difficulties they have been warned to expect. In the sections that follow, some of the problems that arise in developing joint programs will be explained, particularly those of defining and maintaining academic standards, financial structures, and the new roles and relationships that emerge.

The high school principal, probably more than any other official, can most affect the quality and characteristics of cooperative programs. He or she is in the best position to involve school staff, to demonstrate administrative support for the program, to act as a liaison between the school and university or college, and to determine the quality of the program and the academic relationship it creates. Without the active support and involvement of the high school administration, the authors feel that cooperative programing has little chance of succeeding.

To help prepare high school administrators for their leadership role, in the following pages we will discuss important issues, illustrate current activities, review some procedural and evaluative matters, and suggest how to get started and whom to ask for help. We will share some of our experiences during the last five years in developing one such program—Syracuse University Project Advance (SUPA). We are using this model for illustration, not because it is inherently better than other

1

designs, but because it is a model with which we have had extensive first-hand experience and because it allows us to offer a *specific* context in which to discuss such questions as the following:

- What is the historical basis for the problem of poor curriculum coordination between schools and colleges? What workable models of school-college cooperative programs exist? (Chapter One)
- How can such programs be funded during periods of "tight money"? What are the incentives for high school teachers and college professors to make a cooperative program successful? How are responsibilities and roles defined? What kinds of problems can you "count on" and how can you prepare to deal with them? (Chapter Two)
- What kinds of evaluation activities need to be built into a cooperative program to address typical concerns of parents, students, and college officials? (Chapter Three)
- What criteria can be used to make judgments about the quality of existing or proposed articulation arrangements? (Chapter Four)

The rest of Chapter One will review some of the history of articulation programs and will consider present thinking about them. To establish joint programing, principals and superintendents usually have to begin by convincing fellow administrators, school board members, teachers, and parents that the advantages of the program are worth the expense and effort of implementing it. Here is where historical background is essential. It helps us to understand how the problem began and how it might be resolved. We need, in other words, some historical perspective on the problem, a rationale for taking action, and some idea of what practices have proven to be effective and why.

Background

From the mid-1950s to the present, secondary schools have generally encouraged academically capable students to take heavy course schedules, primarily to provide them with intellectual challenge and to permit them to accelerate through required course work. Such programing has not been without certain drawbacks, however. Students, for example, may enter their senior year with few, if any, course requirements left to complete; and, although theoretically they can enroll in electives and other activities that may interest them, many do not. Instead they may spend most of their senior year idly marking time while looking forward to college.

Leaving high school after three or three-and-one-half years may be one solution to senior year boredom, but this option may not be desirable for the majority of students. In addition, it may actually be injurious to the secondary schools (Bowen, 1973). High school administrators, for example, are not happy about losing many of their better students, a loss that can adversely affect the academic climate of the schools, cause stimulating programs and activities to be eliminated, threaten teaching positions, and even reduce state and federal aid.

Many parents, moreover, prefer that their 16-year-old sons or daughters not leave the community so soon, and urge the high schools instead to "beef up" the senior year so that the students will be intellectually stimulated and at the same time be able to enjoy important nonacademic benefits of the senior year: the extracurricular activities and camaraderie that traditionally are part of the last year and which are lost with early graduation.

Responding to the needs of more advanced learners, high schools typically added courses that once were strictly the domain of the university, e.g., calculus and advanced biology. Paradoxically, this initiative has created a particularly frustrating situation for the student, namely, considerable duplication of college work.

Curriculum Duplication

The first year of college for many students is an experience analogous to that of a patient who has to undergo an expensive, complicated, and uncomfortable series of medical tests because the physician does not have the results of earlier tests; does not trust the results of earlier tests; does not believe the patient has already passed them; believes that repeating the tests cannot hurt the patient; and knows that he or she will be paid even if the patient is not. While some may doubt whether this actually happens in the medical profession, no one doubts that it is a frequent occurrence with college freshmen. A good deal of evidence suggests that more and more students are encountering a frustrating amount of course duplication during their last two years of high school and first two years of college (Carnegie Commission, 1973; Casserly, 1965; Snyder, 1975).

Duplication is probably inevitable and even desirable, especially when the material is re-examined on a higher level, and some may be necessary as more students needing remediation are admitted to college. Curriculum duplication, however, is far greater for the above average and superior student than for those with poorer academic records (Eurich & Scranton, 1960). Such duplication often occurs completely by chance rather than purposefully.

Osborn (1928) showed that 17-23 percent of high school physics, English, and history were repeated in college. Russell (1940) found that on the average a person with a B.A. in English will have studied Shakespeare's *Julius Caesar* four times during his total school program. In 1952, a study of curriculum in six high schools and six colleges showed evidence of questionable duplication, wasted time, and damage to student interest and academic motivation in the areas of history, literature, and particularly in the sciences (General Education in School and College, 1952).

A more recent study by Blanchard (1971) evoked considerable interest in the educational community. He found in an extensive survey of college and high school curriculum practices that nearly one-third of the subject matter during the first two years of college was merely a repetition of what had already been taught in high school. That is, one-third of the content of the four areas of the college curriculum (English, math, science, and social studies) was judged by high school and college teachers participating in the study to be nothing more than "high school courses rearranged into a college course and then offered under a new name, but unmistakably continuing as high school substance" (Blanchard, p. 17).

Until better channels of communication develop so that high schools and colleges can arrive at some consensus on curriculum planning, such unplanned duplication and misuse of time and resources will probably continue.

General Education—Whose Responsibility?

Increasingly, educators are beginning to feel that high schools can start to assume more responsibility for the general education courses which currently make up much of the student's first two years of college. This is partly due to the changing nature of the student population. Research suggests that most students are more advanced physiologically, intellectually, and academically than were their counterparts a generation ago and that many entering college freshmen are often particularly advanced in the field of general education (Magill, 1973; Fleischmann Commission, 1973).

Improvement in many academic areas may actually have occurred when schools, responding to a more mature learner and trying to strengthen their college preparatory curriculum, added courses that were once strictly the domain of colleges (e.g., calculus, psychology, sociology, economics, statistics).

Many teachers and students at both the high school and college levels (Blanchard, 1971; Carnegie Commission, 1973) feel that the instructional-social settings offered by the secondary schools may be more conducive to the teaching-learning process in general education than those presently offered by the colleges.

Crowley (1942) cites as reasons for favoring such a shift the lack of interest among many college faculties particularly university faculties in this area of teaching (far too few take freshman and prefreshman instruction seriously), the dominant status of the research function, and the frequent emphasis on special rather than general education. De Vane (1964) reported that moving more of the responsibility for developing basic competence in English composition and in foreign languages to the high school would probably benefit higher education.

Many feel that the needs of both the advanced college-bound learner and the student who needs remediation could best be served in the more protective, cajoling, and prodding high school environment (Sizer, 1973) than in that of the college, which often presumes greater student independence.

Economic Considerations

Other factors dramatizing the need to create better articulation are those that relate to the economic aspects of inadequate coordination between school and college. Using 1965-66 figures, Blanchard (1971) calculates that because of overlapping subject matter nearly three million freshmen and sophomores enrolled in public and private institutions of higher education are paying tuition and required fees of over $420 million for course content for which their parents have already reimbursed the state during their child's secondary education.

At a meeting of the Upper Midwest Association for College Registrars and Admissions Officers, Nelson (1972) noted that legislators are becoming increasingly concerned about the rising costs of education and are not happy about any waste or slippage. With new forms of higher education gaining recognition (e.g., University Without Walls, private occupational degree), colleges—if they are to survive—must find ways to serve better the large student population that currently chooses these proliferating options (Nelson, 1972; New York State Department of Education, 1974).

In New York State alone, in addition to 215 colleges and universities, there are 299 private occupational schools, 46 private business schools, and 34 correspondence schools, with total enrollments of more than 250,000 (Regents of the University of the State of New York, 1974). As the cost of education multiplies, state and federal legislators are tending to view education as a single budgetary package and are demanding more rational coordination of various components of the system.

In short, there is growing support for the position that *college-level instruction should be offered by institutions best equipped to do so and when students are ready for it. Such instruction should occur in the setting best suited to its success and should be provided by those most interested in and capable of doing it. When instruction in certain academic areas is handled adequately by the secondary school, it makes little sense economically, ethically, or educationally to repeat that instruction in college.*

In light of such obvious need to articulate secondary and post-secondary education, why, then, has such cooperation in instructional planning been relatively rare?

First, historically there has been little incentive for schools and colleges to work together. High schools and colleges developed as separate, self-contained components of the larger educational system (Pincus, 1974). Even community colleges, which were, in many cases, connected to secondary schools, have sought to separate themselves from such ties in their quest for recognition (Gleazer, 1973).

Universities have traditionally emphasized research that would extend the fund of learning and have insisted that there be no compromise of rigorous thinking and scholarly inquiry. They have often faulted secondary school personnel for what they regard as short-sightedness in handling problems and casualness about verifying results. High schools, on the other hand, have tended to see university people as minimizing many practical considerations involved in implementing complicated theories. These different perspectives have, at least in part, been responsible for breeding mutual distrust.

Another consideration is the marked difference in organizational climate between the university and the high school, a difference which has been described as "cool vs. intense" (Tom, 1973). University faculty members generally have intermittent teaching assignments; they often have private office space, time, and facilities to do research; and considerable control over their daily schedules. Public school teachers, on the other hand, usually have their workday booked to capacity, have almost no private space, and seldom have opportunity for planning and research. Problems of communication between the two often stem from differences in their professional teaching environments, other considerations aside.

Development of New Options

Educators have been aware for some time of the need for careful sequencing of instruction and of the variety of ways in which curriculum practices can affect learning (Bruner, 1960). The instructional autonomy that characterizes American education, however, has resulted in no single educational sector taking responsibility for dealing with overall problems of instructional continuity and planning. Only recently have the means been developed to encourage timely student movement within and among institutions, and these have been created largely because of pressures from an increasingly diverse student population and from tightening economic circumstances.

7

The problems of school-college articulation are not new; neither is advocacy for reform. The Carnegie Commission on Higher Education (1973), for example, has recommended that better guidance services be developed and that there be more individually tailored programs in the freshman year of college. The Commission has also urged that greater use be made of advanced standing for qualified students.

The National Commission on the Reform of Secondary Education (Brown, 1973) has recommended a movement away from the Carnegie Unit as a standard for academic credit and has also urged that more credit be awarded for experiential learning. The Fleischmann Commission Report (1973) also discusses a variety of new options for high school students.

These various commission reports, however, do not specifically address the considerable technological and logistical problems involved in operationalizing their recommendations. They do not, for instance, consider very closely how the recommended activities are to be financed or how to assess student achievement while maintaining academic quality.

Nevertheless, there are programs and practices developed in recent years that do alter traditional time requirements for degrees, do award credit for experiences gained outside the college classroom, and do allow colleges and high schools to work together to develop transitional options of their own. Some of them are working effectively within existing fiscal and procedural constraints. Many of them are also, in one way or another, challenging traditional patterns and practices. Time-shortened degree programs, credit-by-examination, and various inter-institutional curriculum articulation programs all represent new relationships between institutions and their learners.

Models for Curriculum Articulation

In light of the circumstances and forces that have worked against cooperation, it is encouraging to note a variety of successful new joint school-college programs. A fairly recent survey (Wilbur, 1975) reveals several interesting new articulation arrangements as well as a number of effective and imaginative uses of options that have been available for some time. "Curriculum articulation" is used in this publication to refer to "cooperative programs and practices linking secondary and post-secondary curricula." The curriculum articulation programs surveyed by Wilbur (1975) and noted in the review of literature can be organized within the conceptual scheme indicated in Table 1.

Table 1

Four General Models of School-College
Curriculum Articulation Arrangements

Teaching Responsibility	Course Design	
	Special Design	Regular Catalog
College Faculty	A	B
High School Faculty	C	D

Programs in all four cells of the matrix generally have at least two characteristics in common:

- Recognition that some high school students are capable of real achievement in college courses.
- Assumption that certain high school students can and should be allowed to earn college credit or eligibility for advanced placement by participating in cooperative school-college programing.

The first category of program design, Cell A, includes programs in which college faculty, often in conjunction with high school representatives, design special programs of study for advanced high school students. Faculty from the college, as indicated in the matrix, are responsible for classroom instruction. Among such programs are special college programs which allow high school students simultaneously to complete requirements for graduation and many of their initial college courses. Other programs are designed to operate in the high school as part of a student's elective program.

Cell B of the matrix includes programs whose design involves regular college catalog courses being taught by college faculty to non-matriculating high school students. Perhaps the most common type of cooperative program, this design creates opportunities for high school students to take college courses, either in their high school or at a nearby campus, for college credit while still enrolled in high school. Often referred to as a "split-day" arrangement (Bremer, 1968), this cooperative programing allows academically able students to interact with college professors, experience college-level course requirements, and earn credit applicable toward both high school graduation and baccalaureate degrees. (For descriptions of various programs, see "College Courses: A Twelfth Grade Option," NASSP *Curriculum Report*, December 1975.)

Programs falling in Cells C and D share a basic underlying assumption: *that colleges recognize the ability of high school students to complete college work successfully while they also recognize the capability of some high school teachers to teach college-level course content* (Lindsay, 1965). This basic premise seems to account for many of the differences in program design. Bremer (1968) argues that articulation programs not "high school-focused" deny that the high school has the ability to present a college-level course. The result, he observes, is that the college, rather than the high school, becomes the focal point of acceleration and assumes the instruction-evaluation role. Secondary schools, therefore, serve merely to identify students whom they feel are capable of participation.

A number of other programs are included in the third area, Cell C. High school faculties are responsible for teaching college-level courses. Standardized testing programs (e.g., College Level Examination Program, Advanced Placement) often involve specially designed courses of study that result in norm-referenced scores or ratings for which increasing numbers of post-secondary institutions are granting course exemption, both with and without college credit (College Entrance Examination Board, 1974). Other cooperative experiments involve high school and college faculties designing courses that are also taught by the high school faculty and carry college credit.

Type D programs are by far the least common of the four categories of articulation practices, and represent a major breakthrough in school-college relationships. In general, such programs give high school students an opportunity to earn college credit for regular college courses taught in the high school by selected high school teachers. Usually, courses carry credit which is applicable toward high school graduation and is transferable to post-secondary institutions for credit or advanced placement toward degree requirements. Programs in this category require special administrative structures and strong commitment to evaluation if they are to succeed. This type of cooperative venture—*regular college courses taught in the high school using existing facilities and staff but supervised by a faculty from a sponsoring college or university*—is the primary focus of this monograph.

This chapter presented a rationale for having high school seniors enroll in college courses and for enabling high school and college faculties regularly to work together. In the next chapter we will discuss ways to actually implement school-college cooperative programs and, further, to develop procedures, staffing, and administrative structures that will create and preserve successful working relationships among the cooperating institutions. Chapter Two will use Syracuse University Project Advance as the primary illustrative model because it is a cooperative program of proven success whose development has been fully documented.

2. Establishing and Maintaining Cooperative Programs

AN IDEA MAY SPRING from almost any source, but it is not likely to become more than an idea unless it answers a felt need and receives the support of people who have the knowledge and power to turn it into a reality.

The idea of school-college cooperative programs has been around for some time, but most attempts to implement it have either failed or survived only as transient experiments. If Syracuse University's Project Advance has so far met with a kinder fate, it is probably because the program was created in response to an urgently felt educational need and because it received high-level institutional support from people able to enlist the aid of experts.

On several occasions during the 1972 summer vacation, superintendents and principals from seven Syracuse area high schools* met to discuss informally their discontent with programs in their schools for college-bound high school seniors. They discovered that declining academic motivation and senior-year boredom were problems common to all schools represented, particularly among students planning to enter college. They also found themselves under increasing pressure to ameliorate the situation and provide some educational alternatives for students who were either electing early graduation or retrogressing academically.

With these common concerns, they approached John Prucha, vice chancellor for academic affairs at Syracuse University, described the situation to him, and asked him if there was anything the university could do to help. Prucha agreed with their observations and shared their feeling that some solution should be worked out cooperatively. He asked Robert M. Diamond, director of the University's Center for Instructional Development, to meet and work with the high school administrators. Out of these meetings came a list of characteristics that

*Participants were Fritz Hess and John Vona of East Syracuse-Minoa School District; Richard McGee and Rodney Wells, Jamesville-Dewitt; David Darsee and Edward Pasto, Fayetteville-Manlius; Ted Wodzinski and Donald Yates, Lewiston-Porter; Robert Capone, John Gunning, Ernest Rookey, Patrick Spadafora, and James Zathukal, Syracuse School District.

a cooperative program would require in order to answer the needs of the high schools.

Among the characteristics were the following:

- *High school seniors should be able to enroll in college credit courses that would be offered in the high school building.* Students could already take courses at a local campus during the school day, but the time and costs of commuting and the difficulty in coordinating schedules were among the disadvantages seen with this option; hence the request to keep the courses, if possible, in the high school.

- *The courses would be taught by existing high school staff.* Again, it was already possible to bring the faculty from nearby colleges into the high school to teach the college courses, but there were two problems with this: First, it was unnecessary since many high school faculties were already well qualified to teach college courses (they were experienced teachers, often with master's degrees plus 30 to 45 credit hours, and many had taught in the evening and summer divisions of local post-secondary institutions); second, bringing in outside personnel, especially when enrollments were declining and there were pressures to reduce staff, might be resented by teachers' unions.

- *Credit earned in these courses should be widely transferable to colleges and universities around the country.* However the program might evolve, it couldn't be just a feeder program for Syracuse University. Credit earned would have to be certified and the program conducted so that it would be accepted at most other colleges and universities. Transferability of credit would be an important factor in motivating high school students academically and helping them obtain placement in college programs appropriate to their achievement.

Diamond and several members of his staff carefully considered the schools' requests along with concerns voiced by university faculty who were asked to comment on results of the preliminary meetings. A plan for joint programing was presented to the high schools by the university in the spring of 1973. The proposed program was called Syracuse University

Project Advance and had essentially the same features as the present version. The number of districts interested in participating in the pilot program expanded to six, for a total of nine high schools and approximately 400 students. Details of program funding, staffing, administration, course development, and teacher selection and training will be discussed later in this chapter.

Why should a university bother to enter into such a relationship with the secondary schools, particularly when the institution will probably realize no income nor any great influx of students?

One reason is that most colleges and universities, whether public or private, are under a good deal of pressure to respond to community needs and in other ways generate a favorable public image. Particularly where a problem has received extensive publicity, university officials are hard pressed to "look the other way" when secondary school officials or influential members of the community make a well-articulated and reasonable request for assistance.

The opportunity, for example, to directly influence the quality of the English composition program of high school seniors, some of whom will arrive on campus the following year, is one that many college professors interested in curriculum development would eagerly accept. Moreover, if the joint program is a success and the students and their parents associate the sponsoring college or university with an improvement in school programing, then the institution may actually attract new or better students regardless of efforts to ensure wide portability of the credits.

Some readers may say, "Fine. It worked at your institution, but, although the people I've talked with at the local college acknowledge the importance of the problem, that's about as far as they go. Few suggestions and no action."

If there's one thing to be learned from the early history and later success of SUPA and many other joint programs around the country it is that, from the beginning, there was administrative support at high levels for the project. People in positions of power must convince others at their institution that the concept is important and that a program can be developed that will benefit them. Such people have to rally the support of the faculty, deal with their questions and concerns, and provide the necessary incentives for their assistance. Further (and very important), their help and wisdom are needed in selecting suitable college staff who will ultimately work with the schools.

Some suggestions for identifying such a campus advocate follow:

- Try to determine the reasons for the initial resistance and see if workable solutions have been developed by sponsors of other cooperative programs (e.g., ways of assuring the maintenance of academic standards on and off campus, effective methods of selecting and training teachers, ways to finance the program without additional expenditures by the college).
- Contact another segment of the college or university administration (e.g., member of the board of trustees or alumni organization).
- Organize support among leaders in surrounding area high schools to demonstrate to the college the extent of the problem and to explore all possible lines of contacts and relationships developed with members of the college community by members of the school group.
- Attempt to enlist the support of a staff member on a college campus that is currently sponsoring joint instruction with high schools to speak to some of the concerns raised by administrators or teachers at your local college.
- Seek assistance from the appropriate agency in your state's department of education. Advocacy both in the form of position statements encouraging high school-college cooperative programing and seed monies for pilot efforts from the department of education have been very important in New York State.

Without solid administrative support for cooperative programs in both the schools and colleges, little hope exists for getting beyond the discussion stage.

Legal Considerations

Once there is a preliminary commitment to go ahead with designing a cooperative program, many details have to be worked out that will determine the quality and durability of the rela-

15

tionship. One of the very first matters that must be checked is the legality of various aspects of the proposed college program.

Under state guidelines is it, for instance, possible to charge students tuition for instruction offered in high school buildings? Are the high schools obliged to supply instructional materials for students participating in such college-credit-bearing courses or may the students be asked to purchase various items? May students earn dual credit, that is, high school as well as college credit for the same course? Must the college courses be open to students who are only interested in receiving high school credit? Can the high school or college establish admission prerequisites for these courses whether or not the student is seeking college credit? How are the tuition monies collected from students to be handled?

In each state and for each program both the legal questions asked and the answers given by state department legal counsel will probably differ. In the case of Project Advance, Thomas Sheldon, then deputy commissioner for primary, secondary, and continuing education in the New York State Education Department, advised that:

- First and foremost, courses offered through Syracuse University Project Advance were to be considered regular high school course offerings and subject to all the laws pertaining to such courses including the obligation by the high school to supply necessary instructional materials at no cost to the student.
- It was legal for students who wished to enroll in the courses to pay tuition to Syracuse University, providing there was a direct financial relationship between Syracuse University and the student (i.e., checks for tuition were made payable to Syracuse University).
- Any high school student with the proper subject prerequisites must be allowed to enroll in the college courses whether or not he or she chooses to seek college credit; students seeking college credit may receive separate college and high school grades and credit.
- The official status of Project Advance participants would be *full-time high school students* for all legal purposes. As far as their university status, they would be considered *part-time, nonmatriculating students.*

Try to anticipate all important legal considerations before launching the program. Document in writing all legal matters and work to establish a good contact in your state's education department whom you can regularly turn to for opinion and advice.

Funding and Long-Term Planning

When Syracuse University Project Advance was still only a vague concept, we tried to determine how joint school-college programs typically got started financially and what patterns of financing were associated with successful efforts and with those that ultimately were terminated. We found that most projects were assisted at the beginning with "seed money" from a foundation or state or federal agency. However, we observed that, while the availability of such monies was an important incentive to begin joint programing, interest waned and projects faltered when such funds were no longer available.

Both the university and high school representatives working on the project decided, therefore, to try to establish a self-supporting budget base that was not dependent upon the university for funds or the changing priorities of outside sponsors. Not requiring a continuing financial commitment by the university also meant less worry about realizing a return for its dollars invested (e.g., profit from student tuitions or sizable numbers of new applicants). If the main investment of the sponsoring institution is its reputation, then the faculty and administrators of the program can turn their full attention toward establishing and maintaining good relationships with the schools and communities and ensuring that the program is academically excellent.

This is not to imply that grants from various sources are not useful or welcomed. Indeed, during the pilot year of Project Advance the New York State Education Department assisted in the costs for inservice training for teachers, instructional materials, and program evaluation.

New York's Board of Cooperative Educational Services (to which many of the state's public schools jointly contribute support) also assisted with some costs of evaluation and teacher preparation. The university itself contributed manpower (administrative coordinators and secretarial assistance

17

Table 2

Budget Categories To Be Considered in Determining the Financial Structure of a School-College Cooperative Program

Possible costs for participating high schools

Major Categories	Subcategories	Comments
1. Inservice workshops	Shared costs by districts Teacher salaries	Costs involved with inservice teacher training including salaries of college faculty, overload compensation to teachers, instructional materials, administrative coordination, etc.
2. Instructional materials	Initial purchases Expendables and replacements	Textbooks, audiovisual equipment and supplies, laboratory materials, evaluation instruments, course syllabi, etc.
3. Travel	Mileage Train or air fare Meals and lodging	Travel costs to and from periodic meetings, seminars, and workshops
4. Personnel costs	Substitutes Load adjustments	Substitutes for teachers attending seminars or workshops, costs of possible teaching/duty load adjustments for faculty responsible for certain college courses.

Possible costs for sponsoring college or university

1. Salaries and benefit costs for administrative personnel	Program director	Program coordination and policy formation. Course and program development, evaluation and revision, material production and correspondence, management of student records; liaison with college or university registrar
	Course development and evaluation Secretarial Student records clerk	
2. Registration and transcripts	Record keeping and reproduction	Grade reports and transcripts; payment for college or university administrative services
3. Printing, duplicating, and instructional materials preparation	Photocopying Printing and preparation Audiovisual services Graphics and editing	Services for instructional and program material design and production
4. Travel	Train, car, and air transportation Meals and lodging	Travel costs for program supervision for administrators and faculty
5. Scholarships		Tuition assistance for needy students, provisions for student tuition assistance
6. Office	Telephone Rental of office space and utilities Equipment rental, purchase, and maintenance Computer and data processing services Office supplies	General miscellaneous expenses

on a part-time basis) and instructional materials; officials also made available telephones, meeting rooms, and printing facilities. Such assistance, particularly during the conceptual stage and pilot period, is important since many schools lack the extra resources (outside of carefully budgeted categories) to purchase a large block of new instructional materials for a single course or contribute to regional training institutes for teachers.

The point is that a program should not depend too much on such continued assistance even if it is initially available. Schools should not be diverted from their goals because of the chance for outside cash. If principals depend too much on outside funding, they will simply find it more difficult to achieve self-reliance.

The type and size of budget that is constructed depends upon the characteristics and size of the program. Some of the possible budget categories and their justification are indicated in Table 2.

Many of the categories (e.g., faculty supervision, administrative support services) shown in Table 2 are discussed further in later sections of this chapter. You can obtain specific assistance in budget development from current administrators of various cooperative projects listed in the Appendix.

Course Selection and Development

When considering the type and design of college courses to be offered in high schools, it is a good idea to keep in mind the basic objectives of joint programing. A high school-college cooperative program should provide students with an instructional experience that will stimulate them academically, give them a solid and realistic college experience, smooth the transition between high school and college, and offer them academic credit that is transferable to a wide variety of colleges. A cooperative program like Project Advance enjoys an additional advantage over programs less intimately associated with high school teachers. It requires high school and college faculties regularly to work together on curriculum matters of mutual concern, a collaboration that fosters a sense that Project Advance is not something apart from their schools, but something that is a part of their schools. Keeping these ends in view, the high school principals and university officials who established Project Advance decided to concentrate on general education courses (e.g., math, science, social studies, and English) that had undergone several years of systematic instructional development on campus.

These courses were chosen for several reasons: First, research has shown that courses such as English, calculus, biology, and history are the most poorly articulated academic areas between high school and college; that is, they contain the greatest amount of unplanned duplication of content, which represents a poor use of student and institutional time and resources. Second, since they are foundation courses in nearly all college programs, students are eager to take them to help ensure their success in college and so that they may take more advanced and challenging courses as college freshmen. Third, there are many more academically qualified and experienced high school teachers who can teach the general education courses than can teach courses of the professional school or elective type.

Over the years Project Advance has also offered courses outside the standard general education core. A music course focusing on brass instruments, a course on comparative religion, a drug education course, and a communications course for prospective journalism majors are some of these offerings. Our initial observations about student interest and teacher preparation were confirmed when the religion, drug education, and communications courses were dropped because of lack of student interest in enrolling in them and because it was difficult to find experienced and qualified high school instructors to teach them.

Another common characteristic of Project Advance courses is that they have undergone extensive on-campus instructional development, a process that enabled us to transfer the courses to the high school setting without too much difficulty. The Center for Instructional Development, mentioned earlier as the parent organization of Project Advance, has worked with various departments and colleges on campus to improve instruction by redesigning university courses. This instructional development process, in simple terms, asks a course instructor working with an instructional developer to do the following:

21

- Specify to the extent possible the learning objectives of the course;
- Select or create a course design and instructional materials that will fulfill the learning objectives;
- Produce tests and other evaluation instruments to measure learning, student attitudes, etc.;
- Resolve logistical problems of teaching the course;
- Pilot test the course and field test instructional materials;
- Revise the course and instructional materials where necessary; and
- Continue the process as circumstances change in order to maintain course vitality.

The instructional development process, originally applied to improve campus course instruction, later enabled us to transfer these courses to a high school setting and at the same time preserve college standards. It enabled us to validate claims made for the courses that are implicit in the fact that their successful completion earns Project Advance students college credit reported on a regular university transcript.

What exactly are these claims?

Project Advance courses are college courses identical in every important respect to their on-campus counterparts: the learning objectives, tests, instructional materials, course work, and grading standards are the same, and the course design is comparable. Research and evaluation have shown that Project Advance students perform as well as, if not better than, on-campus students taking the same courses and receiving the same grades. In other words, universities asked to accept Syracuse University Project Advance credit can be assured that P.A. students who have earned passing grades in these courses will have earned at least those same grades on campus.

Since the instructional development process is so important to the validation of Project Advance courses, we should perhaps take a closer look at it. The Center for Instructional Development employs a number of highly qualified development and evaluation specialists and various support services and personnel (e.g., printing, editing, graphics, photography, and audiovisual) in redesigning courses. These resources are utilized during the instructional development process (see Figure

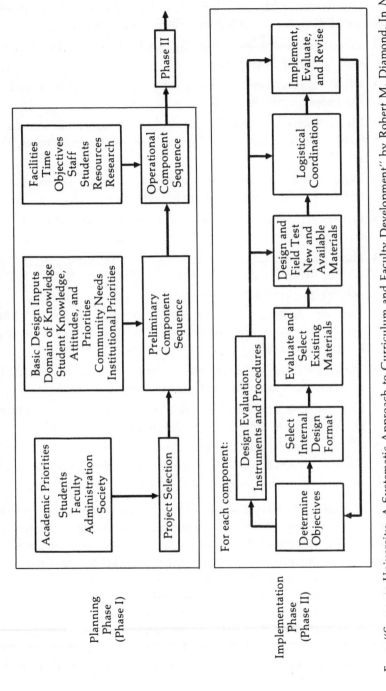

Figure 1
Process Model for Instructional Development

Planning Phase (Phase I)

Academic Priorities
Students
Faculty
Administration
Society

Project Selection

Basic Design Inputs
Domain of Knowledge
Student Knowledge, Attitudes, and Priorities
Community Needs
Institutional Priorities

Preliminary Component Sequence

Facilities
Time
Objectives
Staff
Students
Resources
Research

Operational Component Sequence

Phase II

Implementation Phase (Phase II)

For each component:

Design Evaluation Instruments and Procedures

Determine Objectives

Select Internal Design Format

Evaluate and Select Existing Materials

Design and Field Test New and Available Materials

Logistical Coordination

Implement, Evaluate, and Revise

From "Syracuse University: A Systematic Approach to Curriculum and Faculty Development" by Robert M. Diamond. In *New Directions for Higher Education*. No. 15, Autumn 1976, *A Comprehensive Approach to Institutional Development* (William H. Bergquist and William A. Shoemaker, issue eds.). San Francisco: Jossey-Bass, Inc., 1976. Reprinted with permission.

1). This model helps ensure that important questions and considerations are addressed before and during the development process. Examples of such concerns are listed below:

- What courses seem most in need of instructional redesign? (Identify priorities)
- What faculty members should be most heavily involved in the redesign process?
- Ideally, what should the curriculum or course design look like? Realistically, how closely can we approximate the ideal?
- What are the characteristics of the students served (their entering skills, needs, and attitudes)?
- Generally, what are students supposed to learn in the course?
- How important is it that the course be confined to the normal semester calendar? Can we allow time to vary while achievement remains constant?
- Can we diagnose entering skills and deficiencies of students and start the students at different points in the course sequence?
- What kind of management system can we construct to monitor individual student progress through the course?
- Can we use our facilities, teaching staff, and community resources more effectively in the new course design?
- How can we build an evaluation system to gather feedback from students and teaching staff about what aspects of the new design work or do not work?

Although the instructional development model used to redesign all the courses is the same, each course has unique features. The introductory calculus course, for example, allows students to progress at varying rates, depending on their performance on unit examinations. Students are expected to demonstrate mastery of each calculus unit before proceeding to the next sequentially ordered unit. Students are not penalized for failing to pass any particular examination. Instead, the instructor examines the work of students who have done poorly, explains the concepts that are troubling them, gives them additional related assignments, and lets them be retested at a later date. Testing is viewed as an integral part of the learning-teaching process, not simply as a means for assigning grades. The rationale for this approach is based on a desire to keep the level of achievement constant while allowing the time needed to reach that level to vary. The course instructors spend more time assessing and tutoring students than in giving group lectures.

Following the same development process, the freshman English composition course has design features adapted to its own specific conditions. For example, because the course serves such a heterogeneous population the faculty believes that it is important to assess students' entering skills and to start them with appropriate work. Based on the results of a diagnostic examination and a writing sample, students are assigned to advanced or basic writing units or even to remedial work (for which no credit is given). Students are required to complete certain basic units (material the faculty believes every student should know) and then are allowed to choose literature units (called minicourses) and research paper topics from a wide variety of options.

Certain features are common to nearly all courses developed by the Center. For example, wherever possible, students are allowed to move through the course at their own pace rather than being forced to accelerate prematurely or hold back in order to keep in step with the group. Course objectives, grading standards, content coverage, options, and basic requirements are some of the matters carefully specified and fully explained for students in their course manuals. For courses in which there are more than 12 teachers there are also instructors' manuals that provide the teachers with examples and critiques of model student papers, group-endorsed grading standards, instructions for keeping student records, supplemental content material, and so on. In addition, all courses and course components are continually reevaluated to determine how and where improvements should be made. In other words, evaluation is built in and development is continual.

It is not essential that one specific instructional development model be followed during course development (a process, by the way, that never really ends), but it is vital that all college courses implemented in the high school through a cooperative program have a *well-defined rationale and learner objectives, publicly stated criteria for judging learning outcomes, and evidence that materials used in the courses are reliable and valid.*

High school administrators have an obligation to ascertain, for example, that what the student is expected to learn, read, and do, and how the student will be evaluated have been carefully thought out and communicated to the student; that instructional materials used are really effective; and that grading standards are clear enough for the high school teachers to be able to apply them. High school administrators would be wise to make sure that these data about each course are available *before the course is implemented in the high school.* Remember, the college course should be judged on its own merits; its worth should not be presumed solely because it is associated with, or certified by, a college or university.

Teacher Selection and Preparation

In cooperative programs where high school teachers do most or all of the instruction, teacher selection and preparation should be among the most important concerns of the school administrator. The college courses offered in the high school are usually introductory freshman courses designed to prepare students for more advanced courses, but they may be the only courses the student will take in these particular academic areas. It is essential that these first courses be of high quality—a responsibility that falls largely on the instructors.

High school teachers in such a program face another exigency not usually a problem when the courses are taught on campus by college faculty; that is, to maintain credibility with outside colleges and universities that may be asked to accept the credit, there must be assurances that high school teachers are qualified to teach college courses. That there is at least some bias in this credentials challenge must be admitted, especially when we consider that many high school teachers are better qualified to teach introductory college courses than some college teachers to whom the job is usually relegated. Graduate teaching assistants or new Ph.D.s (who often teach these courses) may have little or no teaching experience and minimal interest in teaching a freshman course, yet, because

26

Figure 2

Approximate Timeline and Activities Preceding the Implementation of Syracuse University Project Advance

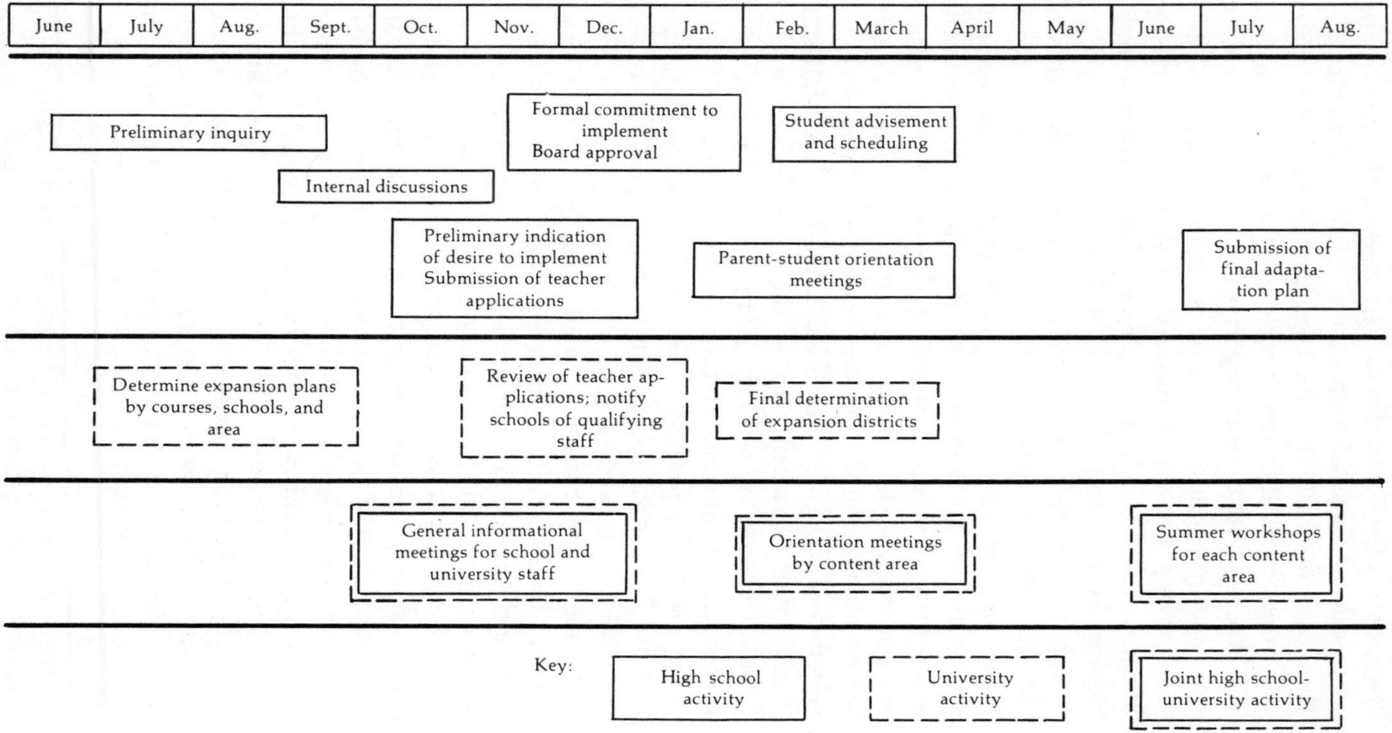

June	July	Aug.	Sept.	Oct.	Nov.	Dec.	Jan.	Feb.	March	April	May	June	July	Aug.

Preliminary inquiry

Internal discussions

Formal commitment to implement Board approval

Student advisement and scheduling

Preliminary indication of desire to implement Submission of teacher applications

Parent-student orientation meetings

Submission of final adaptation plan

Determine expansion plans by courses, schools, and area

Review of teacher applications; notify schools of qualifying staff

Final determination of expansion districts

General informational meetings for school and university staff

Orientation meetings by content area

Summer workshops for each content area

Key:

High school activity

University activity

Joint high school-university activity

they are "college" teachers, their credentials are not challenged as readily as those of high school teachers. Whether or not this should be the case, it is the case, and participants in a cooperative program must be prepared to meet these challenges.

There is another very important reason to have careful selection and preparation procedures. Such procedures help avoid later having to remove unsuitable teachers from the program, a course of action that is almost always painful and embarrassing for everyone involved. When cooperative programs are just getting started there is a tendency for both high school and college administrators to keep teacher selection procedures relaxed and informal. College personnel do not want to seem distrustful of the judgment of their high school counterparts, and high school administrators may be under even more powerful constraints since they have to work regularly with their teachers and would not want to offend them. When teacher selection is left largely to the discretion of the high school administrators, it actually makes their jobs harder by permitting them to choose on a basis other than individual merit. This administrative dilemma recalls Abraham Lincoln's misgivings about political patronage: for every job in his gift there were at least 10 applicants; whatever his choice, he usually made nine enemies and one ingrate!

Whatever the reason, lack of attention to teacher selection almost always results in problems that are difficult to correct. During the first and second years of Project Advance, we relied almost entirely on the recommendations of high school principals for teacher selection. We found that some teachers were chosen chiefly because of their seniority in their departments. Occasionally, and usually in retrospect, we discovered that a principal felt obliged to ask, for example, a department head over a more qualified teacher because it would have been embarrassing to pass over the former. Political reasons were not the only cause of occasional unsuitable choices, however. Sometimes the principal simply did not have enough background information about the prospective course to make an appropriate selection. As a result, some teachers were asked to teach courses for which they felt poorly prepared.

Two years' experience with the program taught us how unwise it is to treat so important a process casually; so, beginning in the third year of Project Advance, we established the following steps for selecting and preparing new teachers and school districts to enter the program. (Figure 2 summarizes these steps and relates them to the academic calendar.)

1. General informational meetings are held in a relaxed setting to acquaint school personnel with each of the course designs they are considering, the associated instructional materials, the nature and duration of summer training sessions for teachers, the type of student each course is designed to serve, and so on. It is a good idea to expose participants to the basic characteristics of the program before this first meeting through written materials. We strongly urge that in addition to teachers and school administrators, guidance and other supervisory staff be present at early meetings to develop a sense of proprietary participation in the program, should it be adopted.* These meetings also enable all parties (e.g., teachers, college faculty, administrators, board members) to get to know one another and to decide whether working together would be enjoyable and beneficial.

2. After the high school has had an opportunity to consider the merits of various college courses and to decide whether it can meet conditions required by the university to offer the program, it is then asked to submit applications for interested teachers who seem to have the academic qualifications and teaching experience stipulated by the university. The applications must be accompanied by copies of teachers' college transcripts and by letters of recommendation from subject area supervisors and principals. In reviewing this information, faculty committees from the appropriate university departments look for extensive teaching experience in the specific content area (usually a minimum of five years); undergraduate and master's degree in the content area (sufficient to qualify

---

The success of cooperative programs in the high school is dependent, among other things, on thoughtful student selection and advisement, the teachers having the necessary time in their schedules for preparation and advising, assistance in the school from other teachers not directly involved in the project, and class scheduling. If the program is identified with a single administrator or associated with a small group of teachers, lack of support and even resistance are almost always encountered.

the instructor to teach at the college or university level); and, in some cases, particular kinds of course work in the teaching of writing. After the committees have reviewed credentials, the high school is notified of their applicants' standing—"approved," "conditionally approved," or "not approved"—for participation in the formal preparatory workshop.

Principals usually submit at least three names in each course area to the university for review so that there will be some flexibility in choosing among qualified staff to send to the summer workshops, assuming that the teachers are approved and that the courses will be taught. Even if not all the teachers who have been selected and trained are immediately involved in teaching the course, they can provide the teacher who is actually teaching it with moral support and serve as back-up staff, should the teacher, for various reasons, be unable to continue in the program.

Although the criteria and procedures for judging teachers' credentials are established chiefly by the sponsoring university, the high school principal remains a very important participant in the teacher selection process. The principal, usually with the appropriate department chairperson, is in the best position to consider significant factors about applicants which are not always apparent from examination of "paper" credentials. They may, for example, help answer the following questions:

—Does the teacher understand the need for, and would he or she be comfortable with, continuing outside supervision of the program by college faculty?

—Does the teacher work well with, and have the respect of, other teachers within his or her department?* (Important for eliciting their support for the program and for promoting desirable spin-offs within the department curriculum.)

---

*Our experience has been that prima donna teachers almost never work well in the program. Often very competent and effective in their own classrooms, they usually relate well to only a few colleagues and strongly resent any intrusion into their classroom activities. Both characteristics foredoom necessary university supervision and harmony within the high school department.

—Given the specific course design, learning objectives, and evaluation procedures that will be used, is the teacher likely to enjoy teaching, and be effective, in the program?

3. After the university notifies the high school principals which teachers have been accepted for the summer training program, all conditions that must be provided to offer the courses for college credit are reviewed. These guidelines, like the teacher selection process itself, have been developed after several years of trial and error. They specify maximum class size, teacher load, required facilities, instructional materials, and class scheduling. Later in this chapter, we will describe in detail the administrative guidelines for Project Advance course offerings and explain how they evolved.

   Students and their parents should be counseled well in advance of student program scheduling for the following academic year. This usually includes information about course designs, prerequisites, grading, credit transfer, costs, type of student the program is designed to serve, and so on.

4. The next step is an all-day course orientation meeting for high school teachers and university faculty in each content area. This meeting is to review the course design in detail, describe the summer training programs (e.g., daily agenda, written proposal requirements, readings), and consider preworkshop activities (e.g., planning orientation meetings for parents and students, ordering instructional materials, class scheduling). The meeting also provides an additional opportunity for high school and college faculty members to get to know each other better, to understand their respective teaching milieus, and to begin building mutual trust to ensure successful collaboration.

5. The final step before actual implementation of the program is the summer workshop for all participating teachers. Each workshop (usually seven to 10 days long) is planned and conducted by the university professors who will be supervising the particular course in the high school and who are themselves teaching the course on

31

campus. The emphasis in the workshop is on the pedagogical problems of adapting a campus-designed course to the high school setting. For example, the Syracuse University freshman English course has design features (self-pacing, alternative instructional tracks, minicourses, remediation, diagnostic testing, etc.) which can be accommodated on campus without much difficulty but which do present problems in a high school setting where one or two teachers may be teaching the course to 25 or 50 students.

In addition to these logistical considerations, the university and high school faculty must agree on procedures and standards for evaluating student papers, an especially difficult task in the English composition course. The workshops also give teachers time to consider how school facilities (such as laboratories, libraries, media centers, and seminar rooms) and community services and programs (such as theater productions, college libraries, and research facilities) can be used to benefit the program. The time can also be used to work out solutions to such problems as lack of flexibility in student scheduling, widely varying entry skills of students, and heavily used classroom space.

A carefully conceived and detailed adaptation plan is produced by each workshop participant and must receive university approval before the course is offered for college credit. Generally, the plan is submitted late in July, which allows the university four or five weeks to study it and to request appropriate clarifications or modifications.

The summer workshops and orientation meetings with university and high school personnel enable everyone involved in the program to build relationships of trust and professional regard that are needed to make a cooperative program work. They also prepare instructors to teach courses that are, in every important respect (e.g., content, instructional sequences, grading standards), identical with their campus counterparts.

Administrative Personnel and Supervisory Faculty

Although high school administrators may have little or no

direct influence on the selection of specific supervisory staff at the sponsoring college or university, it nevertheless may be helpful for them to know how the university staffs and operates its cooperative program. This information can aid them by giving them some idea of how committed the sponsoring institution is to the program and how well prepared it is to serve the high schools. If a sponsoring institution relegates its high school program to recently hired or hired-for-the-occasion instructors and if its program is supervised by campus administrators who are busy with other duties, its cooperative program may not outlive the interest of the particular college professor assigned to work with the high school. On the other hand, if the university has established a special organization whose primary function is to service the cooperative program, then it has manifested a very strong commitment to the program and probably places a premium on its success.

Two types of college personnel are usually involved in the cooperative program: administrative staff, who will provide overall coordination and delivery of program services; and supervisory faculty, who are responsible for maintaining academic standards and continuing course improvement. First, let's consider the administrative personnel. Although in very small cooperative programs (150 to 250 students in five or six high schools near the sponsoring institution) it may be possible for one or two college officials to coordinate supervision and administrative tasks part time, we have found that as the program expands (number and geographic distribution of schools, students, and course offerings) a full-time staff is needed to service the program. The following are brief descriptions of staff positions and responsibilities for Syracuse University Project Advance currently serving 60 high schools.

- *Position:* Program director
  Responsibilities and functions: Chief liaison between the schools and academic departments of the university. Prepares and manages the budget. Hires and supervises administrative office staff. Develops program policy. Coordinates faculty travel to schools. Chief spokesman for the program to all outside groups and institutions (colleges and universities, state education departments, accrediting agencies). Determines priorities for evaluation

and research. Works with high schools that are preparing to enter the program.

- *Position:* Evaluator
  Responsibilities and functions: Develops and coordinates research and evaluation for the program. Provides data on the effectiveness of course materials (i.e., their utility, reliability, and validity) and helps faculty interpret the data so that the materials may be revised appropriately. Develops methodology and collects data to determine the quality and comparability of on- and off-campus (high school) instruction. Coordinates data processing and analysis. Prepares written reports on major research and evaluation findings for in-house and public distribution.

- *Position:* Instructional developer
  Responsibilities and functions: Works directly with university faculty to design and improve courses. Prepares new courses for inclusion in Project Advance. Travels with faculty to assess the quality of high school programs. Helps faculty plan and operate teacher seminars and workshops.

- *Position:* Records clerk
  Responsibilities and functions: Coordinates the collection and processing of all student registrations and grade reporting for the program. Serves as liaison to all student records offices at the university. Develops procedures to integrate accurately and efficiently Project Advance student records into the larger university system. Answers all questions (written or by phone) that students, parents, school officials, or representatives of other colleges may have about Project Advance student records. Designs written materials which explain (often translate) university procedures and legal policies for handling Project Advance student records.

- *Position:* Secretary
  Responsibilities and functions: Types correspondence and coordinates mailings to school administrators and teachers concerning program procedures, site-visit evaluations, seminars, and workshops, and handles general correspondence. Makes travel and facilities arrangements for

faculty and administrative site visits, seminars, and workshops. Prepares typed copy for printing instructional materials, such as student and teacher manuals, evaluation forms, student record sheets, programed booklets, and descriptive literature.

In addition to the preceding staff positions, other personnel and services are necessary at least on a part-time or shared basis. For example, a skilled editor is needed to proof and edit instructional materials and other items for public distribution. The assistance of graphic artists is needed to prepare illustrations, design charts, graphs, etc., for printed or visual materials. During peak work periods (e.g., fall and spring registration) part-time clerical help can be essential. And finally, we have found that outside consultants can bring a different perspective to bear on a particular evaluation and research problem, making it very worthwhile to budget for their services.

What factors seem to characterize college faculty who have been successful working in Project Advance? In our view, the most important attributes seem to be the following:

1. *The faculty member should be well established and stable in his or her position at the university.*

    Since considerable time and effort go into cultivating good teacher-professor relationships, it is important that campus faculty members involved with Project Advance plan to remain at the university for at least three years. This means that it is more desirable to work with tenured senior faculty than with untenured faculty. We have used the phrase "well established" in our description because we feel that the faculty responsible for supervising courses in the high school should know their colleagues well and should be strong enough politically to defend the cooperative high school program against various attacks and criticisms from within the university if or when they do occur.

2. *Faculty members should be well respected within their departments for their subject matter expertise and teaching skill.*

    A faculty member in charge of the off-campus implementation of a university course is serving, in effect, as spokesman for the university and for his or her academic department to a variety of people such as school officials, faculty at other colleges examining transcripts, students, and members of the community. The faculty member's view of the curriculum, particularly in the introductory course area, should be supported by the majority of the department faculty. Because it is necessary to handle skillfully problems and interpersonal relationships on and off campus, this faculty member should have a reputation for maturity and fairness.

3. *The faculty member should enjoy teaching and contact with students.*

   Success in, and enjoyment of, teaching and working with students seem to be important factors for successful faculty supervision of an off-campus program. The college faculty member must be able to empathize with the intense demands made of high school teachers and, at the same time, ensure that the services and instruction provided students are never compromised. Given the choice between strength and interests in research or teaching, the teaching orientation is preferable because it is more suited to the kinds of demands faced in a cooperative program.

4. *The faculty member should show a healthy curiosity about the teaching-learning process and should view instructional development as a continuing process.*

   Our experience has shown that, although a well-developed, validated course design is a necessary starting point for joint high school-college programs, the university faculty member must expect, indeed welcome, comments, criticisms, and suggestions for change and improvements in the course from the adjunct high school faculty and students. Examples of changes that have been made in the Syracuse University freshman English program as a direct result of interaction with the high school instructors are the addition of experienced teachers of composition to tutor on-campus students with various skill deficiencies, greater flexibility in student movement between certain writing units, improvements in diagnostic and criterion-skill examinations, refinement of course manuals, and the creation of teacher manuals and inservice workshops for new instructors.

Careful attention to staffing at the sponsoring institution can mean the difference between a long-term, quality program satisfying to all involved or one that will not weather the first crisis. Clearly articulated services and well-defined staff and faculty responsibilities will also help to minimize problems when a change of personnel occurs. Top level administrators at the college or university can best demonstrate their commitment to the joint venture by doing all in their power to see that an able, sensible, and responsible group is at the helm.

Developing Policies and Procedures

What do you mean my daughter is not going to earn any university credit? We paid tuition, didn't we?
— Mother of a Project Advance student

As the above quote suggests, a new and different educational program can cause confusion. *Policies and procedures are needed to prevent misunderstandings, clarify roles and relationships, establish beforehand a consistent way of dealing with problems, promote efficiency, and define conditions and services.*

Because relatively few people have had any experience managing high school-college cooperative programs, policy has had to be formulated, to a certain extent, piecemeal and in response to various crises. This has been true of Project Advance as well. On the following pages are some examples of policies and procedures developed out of our experience.

Program Evaluation and Maintaining Academic Standards

Since the institution sponsoring the cooperative program certifies the college courses taught in the high schools for college credit, its faculty is responsible for seeing that the course in each location meets established grading standards and that an appropriate instructional environment is provided for the students. Academically the high school offering is considered to be simply another section of a particular course described in the institution's course catalog. If any high school in the cooperative program awards students grades that are belied by students' subsequent college performance, then the reputation of the entire program will be tarnished.

During their supervisory visits to the high schools, Syracuse University faculty members read papers and tests that students had written for their Project Advance courses. Occasionally, the grading standards applied by high school instructors seem to be inconsistent with those explained in the student and teacher manuals, the workshops, inservice seminars, and in written communications. The criteria then have to be reviewed with the teachers to clarify any misunderstandings. Where disagreements in grading standards are a continuing and serious problem, the grades on student papers may be adjusted after the university has reviewed them. As a matter of policy, *where differences cannot be resolved, the decisions of the supervising faculty are final. If basic or continuing (or unresolvable) disagreements about grading criteria are encountered, courses may be withdrawn at the option either of the school or the university. The high school principal will be notified if such a situation is anticipated.*

The previous sentence deserves some elaboration. Since the high school principal is held responsible for the success or failure of instruction, he or she must be kept informed of the status of all college courses offered in the school; but this duty may conflict with the obligation to high school teachers to maintain the confidentiality of their interactions with the supervisory university faculty.

Project Advance has moved in the direction of limiting confidentiality. This policy change was made to prevent minor problems from becoming major ones. Although it is a rare occurrence, sometimes a high school teacher will persistently disregard agreed-to procedures of the program. If the dereliction is shielded by a policy of complete confidentiality, then what could have been limited to a relatively minor problem may become a very serious one. In other words, if the high school principal were informed earlier of what had been going on, the situation could probably have been corrected before it became too serious.

Whatever policy is followed, it should be made clear right from the start, and, if any modification is later required, it too should be clarified to everyone affected. The candid and trusting relationship that must exist between the high schools and university for the cooperative program to succeed requires some forms of evaluation to be shared only with the teacher (e.g., student attitude surveys, pedagogic suggestions). Others, usually more general judgments about the program's status, ways to improve the program (e.g., improved student advising, changes in teachers' schedules and teaching loads, the need for additional resources, different use of facilities, the need to train additional teaching staff), and particularly continuing academic disagreements that could affect the future of the course, must be discussed openly with high school administrators.

On a number of occasions in Project Advance, our desire to prevent a deteriorating situation from reflecting poorly upon a teacher has caused us to minimize difficulties in communicating with principals. Only when a long series of corrective measures failed to produce results was the principal brought in. Experience has taught us that it is inadvisable to keep principals in the dark until a crisis develops; rather, there is a need for their continuing involvement. Hence the following policy toward program evaluation:

A variety of research and evaluation activities reflects our continuing need to assess the effectiveness of instruction in university courses, the maintenance of academic standards, the quality of instructional materials, and the impact of the program upon students and curriculum. Such information is not only vital for continued course improvement but also is necessary for colleges and universities in the process of evaluating the university transcripts of participants. Syracuse University maintains a high level of security on all student data, such as student attitude measures, and their use is strictly limited to the teacher and the Project Advance staff. On-site observation reports of academic standards are designed to be shared with those teachers and supervisory personnel in the public school and the university who share the responsibility for the success of the program.

Transferring Academic Credit

Credit transfer among colleges and universities is a complex process characterized by considerable inconsistency and often seemingly capricious and illogical acceptance policies. Acceptance of transfer credit for course exemption, advanced placement, or toward degree requirements varies considerably among (and even within) institutions, even when the credit is earned by a matriculated student on a college campus, let alone when there is the added complication of off-campus instruction. Transfer credit, in other words, cannot be guaranteed.

The best posture for designers or administrators of a cooperative program is, first, to anticipate questions which other institutions might raise about the program (e.g., teachers' credentials, sufficiency and effectiveness of course design, methods of supervision, comparability with campus instruction) and to prepare convincing responses; second, to help prepare students to handle skeptical or negative responses from college admissions personnel (e.g., provide them with course syllabi to take to their colleges, tell them how to explain their college experiences, offer them the assistance of the sponsoring college or university); and third, to conduct on-going research of how credit earned by students in the cooperative program is received by the colleges and universities that admit these students.

We feel that Project Advance credit has been well-received over a documented three-year period. Of the approximately 75 percent of Project Advance students who returned questionnaires, about 80 percent reported having received credit toward their degrees *and* exemption from comparable required courses; 96 percent of these students reported receiving credit. However, credit transfer has hardly been problem-free. Even where the credit has been accepted at an institution for years without question, new freshman advisers or a change in admissions officers can alter that situation. Such uncertainty in credit acceptance is due to a lack of clear policy at the institution. At other colleges and universities transfer credit acceptance may depend on a student's high school record, on separate decisions by the appropriate academic department in the course content area, or on how badly the institution needs to attract new students.

Some colleges go out of their way to seek necessary information from the high school or sponsoring university if they have questions about recognizing the credit. Others simply place all the burden on the student to explain and justify such nontraditional educational experiences (something most students are hesitant or unprepared to do). Still others may refuse to accept the credit because the course was not taught on a college campus or with regular college staff, refusing to consider the course on its own merits.

We have found that, with persistence and patience, it is frequently possible to get officials to reconsider an initially negative decision. No college official, however, can force any college or university to accept transfer credit, so it is unwise to oversell credit transferability to students and parents in promoting interest in the cooperative program. Credits, of course, are always accepted by the sponsoring university.

Over the years, we have made a concerted effort to document the extent to which Project Advance credit has been recognized by other institutions and the type of recognition accorded it. We have compiled a list of colleges and universities which Project Advance students have attended and which have or have not recognized Project Advance credit. At the top of that list appears the following qualifying statement:

Important—Please Read Carefully

This is a list of colleges and universities that have recognized credit earned by Syracuse University Project Advance participants during the past three academic years.The majority of schools have granted both credit toward degree requirements and exemption from similar required courses; other have recognized SUPA course work for credit or for exemption but not for both. *The fact that a college or university is on this list does not mean that it has a policy of accepting SUPA credit or that it has a future commitment to accept SUPA credit; rather, it indicates that the institution has honored SUPA credit in the past.* Evaluation of SUPA or any other type of transfer credit is always made on an individual basis, usually in conjunction with the student's high school record. College officials usually will not commit themselves to a decision before they have received an official Syracuse University transcript.

In a separate list following the first, institutions are noted which do not appear to accept SUPA credit or do so only in very limited ways. As with the first group, this does not imply permanent policy, but simply reflects present policy, as we understand it.

Many students will be going on to colleges and universities which have not previously received students with SUPA credits. Please be patient. We offer the following suggestions in explaining your transfer credit:

41

1. Make sure that you have requested, and that the college has received, an official Syracuse University transcript of your course work.
2. Let them examine your student manual or course descriptions from the University. A brief description also appears in the official Syracuse University catalog.
3. In describing your experience, emphasize that all SUPA courses are regular Syracuse University courses (e.g., same textbooks, assignments, testing) and courses are taught by high school faculty who hold appointments with the appropriate academic department at the university.
4. If, after you have followed the preceding steps, an official at a college has questions that you do not seem to be able to deal with, then feel free to request assistance by writing to:

   Director
   PROJECT ADVANCE
   Syracuse University
   759 Ostrom Ave.
   Syracuse, N.Y. 13210

   Include in your correspondence the name, title, and address of the official we should contact and the nature of his or her questions.

Although it is probably not possible to eliminate completely the confusion and frustration attendant upon credit transfer, it is possible to document the process accurately as it occurs, prepare students for encounters with people unfamiliar with their college experiences, and see that one or more officials at the institution sponsoring the cooperative program are willing to go to bat for students frustrated in dealing with other college faculty or administrators.

Another topic related to credit transfer is the actual procedure students must use to have the record of their college course work transferred to colleges and universities. These procedures for obtaining transcripts must be carefully explained to students, parents, and high school guidance officers. For example, they must be told where and how students should request a transcript, how much it costs, to whom it should be forwarded, and when during the school year students should request the transcript. It is also advisable to explain the right of access to transcripts. Project Advance's policy manual states the following:

Access to student records is protected by University policy and federal law. Only the individual student may request copies of his/her transcript. In order to safeguard an individual's right to privacy, no transcripts will be sent when the request is made by telephone, telegraph, cablegram, or by any individual other than the student.

Other procedural and policy considerations stem from the geographic distance of the high schools from the sponsoring university, differences in academic calendars, and the dual status (high school and college) of participating students. In coordinating the two systems, special attention must be given to such areas as the following: course registration, payment and refunding of tuition, scholarships, dropping and adding courses, making grade changes and handling "incompletes", library privileges for students and teachers, and handling instructional materials efficiently.

In this chapter, we have discussed the necessary steps to implementing a cooperative program, paying particular attention to initiating relationships, selecting and preparing courses and staff, and developing sensible financial and administrative policies. Syracuse University Project Advance was used to illustrate these matters and to sharpen the reader's awareness of the range of variables which can affect school-college cooperative programs. The next chapter will focus on program evaluation; that is, on ways to gather information systematically for continually improving courses and programs. Evaluation also implies a commitment to course and program validation, to examining what is being done, whether it is working, and whether it is worthwhile.

3. The Role of Evaluation Within a Cooperative Program

E VALUATION NEEDS TO BE an integral part of any high school-college program. Well-conceived and carefully conducted evaluation can ensure quality and contribute to the efficiency of a program. It can help reduce frustrations by identifying problem areas early.

Evaluation is the systematic process of collecting, analyzing, and preparing information regarding educational programs for the purpose of description, determination of worth, and fostering better decisions. Within a high school-college cooperative program evaluation serves three needs:

- It provides information for course and program improvement.

- It provides information for describing and justifying your program to others.

- It provides information for student advising.

All of us are evaluators. We make judgments daily about the worth of things and events that touch our lives. Ultimately, the judgment of whether to sponsor, support, pay for, enroll in, or accept credit from an articulation program rests with the individual. Program personnel cannot make those judgments for others. They can, however, help collect and make available information relevant to those judgments. To do this, a program should have someone on staff whose primary responsibility is coordinating and conducting evaluation activities. Evaluation should be an ongoing process within the program.

Evaluation, however, is not the exclusive domain of a single person. Evaluation activities can and must be conducted by all the project staff—program administrators and faculty as they visit schools, teachers as they work with the material, and students as they do the course work. Each contributes a slightly different view and combination of interests. The evaluator needs to encourage, coordinate, and help piece together the information from colleagues as well as personally gathered information.

While the articulation program may be the primary sponsor of the evaluation, it is only one of the audiences. Many people make decisions that affect the success of a high school-college program. Their needs for information differ widely. Students must decide to enroll in the courses. Officials from many colleges must decide to accept the credit students wish to transfer. The sponsoring college must decide periodically whether to continue the program, and program personnel must make decisions regarding the organization and operation of a program. If evaluation is to be effective, it is necessary to assess carefully who the audiences are, what decisions they face, and what information is relevant to those decisions. Table 3 suggests some of the groups who are the audience of evaluation and some of the decisions they will make.

Table 3

Primary Audiences of Evaluation of High School-College Cooperative Programs

Audience	Decision(s) they will make
Sponsoring college	To support and underwrite the program
Program administrators	To organize and operate the program; course offerings; personnel decisions
High school administrators	To offer the program; benefits to the district
High school teachers	To teach the courses or allow others to teach the courses
Students	To enroll in courses
Parents	To pay for courses
Other Colleges	To accept the credit students earn

In deciding what should be evaluated, the effectiveness of the program in achieving its intended outcomes must be considered. However, most school-college programs involve a large number of people, a web of complex relationships, and a diversity of intentions. It is not enough to examine a program in terms of its originally stated objectives. A great number of things happen during a course and in the overall program that are not anticipated but that are an integral part of the experience of participants and need to be considered in making decisions about the program. An evaluation needs to consider transactions as well as outcomes, intended as well as unintended ends.

A number of questions can be offered that might help organize an evaluation effort. Moreover, they are questions that high school teachers and administrators should ask of *any* program proposed for their school.

1. Are college standards maintained? This issue is essential to the credibility of a program, the academic integrity of the sponsoring institution, and the transferability of the credit students earn.

2. Is the college credit students earn easily transferable to other colleges and universities?

3. What is the impact of the program on the sponsoring institution? Institutions differ widely in their motives for sponsoring a cooperative program, but few are likely to tolerate a program that yields negative consequences.

4. What is the long-term impact of the articulation program on high school students' eventual college experience?

5. Are the instructional materials used in the course effective? Does their pattern of use in the course facilitate learning?

6. How effective is the teaching? What teacher behaviors and course characteristics contribute to desired outcomes of the program?

7. Which students are most likely to earn college credit?

8. What is the long-term impact of the program on the high school curriculum?

The next section discusses each of these questions and describes evaluation strategies to respond to them.

Are college standards maintained?

The essential claim of a cooperative program is that the work students complete in high school for which they receive college credit is indeed college level work. A student receiving exemption and going into a more advanced course in college is expected to have covered the basic material from which he or she was exempted and to be able to handle the more advanced work. If the student cannot do so, the whole program will suffer and may eventually be discredited. An example illustrates the point.

When several Project Advance students asked to have their credit accepted at a midwestern university in 1974 and 1975, they were refused. In the early 1960s, this university had agreed to accept college credit which high school students had earned through a cooperative program in the midwest. When students from that program encountered academic problems, the university's officials became concerned and determined that they would not accept credit earned in this fashion—from this cooperative program or any other. Over 10 years later, their one bad experience continued to influence policy and affect students from other programs.

The most common way of assuring that college standards are maintained is to compare the performance of high school students with that of college students who have just completed the course work. This may be a comparison with college students at the sponsoring institution or it may be a comparison with college students more generally; that choice depends on the claims of the particular articulation program.

When the same course is taught at both the high school and at the college, designing a comparative evaluation can be fairly straightforward. If the content coverage of the course is the same both on and off campus, the evaluator will need to find a valid, reliable, and fair measure or indicator of that achievement. It may be an achievement test carefully developed by the college faculty member and the evaluator; it may be a nationally standardized test relevant to the content coverage of the course. It need not, however, be a formal test. A comparative evaluation might involve outside judges evaluating student portfolios in an art course or comparing student writing samples in an English course. Examples will be offered later in this chapter.

Sometimes, however, students in the high school may be taking a course that is different from the course taught on campus. It may be a course specially designed for the high school or a course designed by someone who no longer teaches on campus. This does not mean that the high school course may not deserve college credit, but only that a comparison of high school and college student achievement needs to be sensitive to the differences in the courses. If the content coverage and emphases of the high school and campus offerings are clearly specified, it may be possible to compare students only on those elements which are common. Alternatively, it might be possible to identify a set of campus courses which, taken together, covers the same or similar content and then involve as a comparison group the students who have been through these courses.

Another approach is to assume that both the course taught in the high school and the one taught on the campus are representative samples of a larger content area, such as chemistry, and that, regardless of the particular introductory chemistry course students took, they should be able to compare favorably on a nationally standardized test of introductory chemistry.

Articulation programs that have high school students going to nearby colleges and enrolling in regular campus courses or, alternatively, that have the professor teaching a section of the course in the high school, appear to avoid the issue of college standards. Unfortunately, that is not the case. It is common to hear representatives of these programs argue that college standards are maintained "because college faculty teach the courses." This is not a valid argument because it confuses an input into the course (the person teaching) with an output (how much students have learned). The issue of whether college standards are maintained should be considered in terms of how much students in this course have learned compared to other college students completing similar courses.

It is essential to the future of high school-college cooperative programing that the work for which students receive college credit be of college quality and that sponsors of these programs be able to demonstrate and verify that quality.

Following are examples of comparative evaluations. The first compares high school and college student performance in freshman English. It was selected as an example because of the methodology employed: Outside judges were asked to read, discuss, and compare student writing samples. The second example compared the performance of psychology students in one articulation program with that of college students completing relevant course work at a number of colleges and universities.

48

A Comparison of the Quality of Papers Written by Students in Project Advance Freshman English with Those Written by Students in Freshman English at Syracuse University

This study was designed to serve two purposes: first, to compare the quality of student writing between the Project Advance and campus courses; and second, to describe the characteristics of passing and failing papers written by Project Advance students. In comparing the quality of papers, the study answered two questions: Were papers written by Project Advance students which received passing grades as good as passing papers written by students on campus? And, Were failing papers written in Project Advance English as poor as papers which were considered failing on campus?

To answer these questions, three judges were asked to describe and compare passing and failing papers written on and off campus. This procedure was conducted once for papers at Level II (Composition) and repeated for papers at Level III (Literature). The judges were not told whether the papers they read were considered passing or failing or whether the student authors were from Syracuse University or Project Advance. The three judges participating in this study all had experience with the teaching materials and procedures that were used by the Syracuse University English Department to teach writing. Two of the three judges were familiar with the goals and designs of English instruction in Project Advance.

In this study, the evaluation staff collected essays from the Syracuse University English Department and the Project Advance teachers. At both Level II and III, papers were collected in each of the following groups:

High School Passing   Syracuse University Passing
High School Failing   Syracuse University Failing

Twenty papers were randomly selected from each of these groups. The random sampling helped ensure that the results would generalize to all the students' efforts. However, in examining the samples, one change was found to be needed. The passing papers collected on campus at Level II during the second semester were primarily from tutor sections which were designed to serve students progressing more slowly. While these papers were "passing," they were not judged to be representative of the quality of campus passing papers overall. To offset this, five of the strongest Level II campus passing papers were selected from the 1974-75 English evaluation and replaced by the five weakest passing papers from the tutor sections. With this change, the new on-campus passing set of papers was judged to be representative of on-campus passing papers in general.

Each group of 20 papers was then randomly separated into two piles of 10 papers each. One pile from each group was presented without identification to each judge for examination. The judges reviewed the papers to decide how the essays in each group were similar to one another and different from those in other groups. They were allowed to use whatever criteria they wished.

At Level II, the judges established eight criteria along which the papers were considered. These included Grammar and Mechanics, Language Competency, Style, Organization, Support, Topic and Thesis, Logic, and Depth of Thought. Judges' comments describing each pile of papers across these criteria are reported elsewhere (Chapman, et al., 1978) but a one-page example is included. (See Table 4.)

After the descriptions of each pile were complete, the three judges were each given a set of 40 papers consisting of the remaining 10 papers from each group (passing and failing, on- and off-campus). These papers had been randomly shuffled together. Again, the source and authorship of these papers were not known by the judges. The judges were asked to sort these 40 papers into four piles according to the earlier descriptions.

Interjudge reliability coefficients were computed, and the reliability of the composite scores (i.e., the sum of the scores assigned by all three judges) was estimated to be .68 using the Spearman-Brown prophecy formula.

The same general procedure was used in examining Level III papers. These papers were critical literary reviews rather than the more personal writing used in Level II. Since these papers were much longer than the other essays, fewer of them could be read in the time allocated for this study. Consequently, the judges were each presented with five papers from each of the four sources. Only papers from the current year were used in this portion of the study.

The judges established six criteria to use in describing Level III papers. These included Topic and Thesis, Support and Logic, Grammar and Mechanics, Diction and Usage, and Style and Organization.

Again at Level III, the characteristics identified by the judges after reading this first set of papers were used to sort a second set of 20 papers. The interjudge reliability using all three judges was .57. However, the ratings of one judge correlated quite low with the ratings of the other two. Since the ratings of the other two judges had a rather high intercorrelation, the interrater reliability was re-computed using only the other two judges. This yielded an inter-rater reliability of .83. Again, this indicates that confidence can be placed in these descriptions as a basis for making decisions about groups of papers.

A Comparison of Student Achievement in Psychology Between Project Advance and Selected Colleges and Universities Using the CLEP General Examination of Psychology

The study investigated whether students earning college credit in high school through Syracuse University Project Advance (SUPA) psychology demonstrated a level of achievement equal to or greater than that of college students in psychology courses at six colleges and universities around the country. The information was thought useful to all colleges asked to accept transfer credit from this SUPA course, because it could assure them that students' level of achievement in SUPA corresponds to the achievement of students at their institutions.

At the end of the fall semester of 1976, 698 college students at six institutions and 371 high school students enrolled in SUPA psychology in nine high schools completed the CLEP General Examination in General Psychology.

The colleges participating in the study included C. W. Post College (Long Island), College of St. Benedict (Minnesota), University of Georgia—Athens, University of North Carolina at Chapel Hill, State University of New York at Cortland, and Syracuse University. At the same time, students' psychology course grades were collected and matched with their CLEP scores.

The CLEP Examination of General Psychology was designed to cover the amount of material usually included in a one-semester college course. This test is probably the most widely recognized nationally standardized measure of achievement in psychology. The CLEP exam seemed appropriate to this study because over 1,800 colleges and universities already use student scores on this exam as the basis of placement and/or exemption.

Moreover, CLEP is the only exemption program that offers national norms (Willingham, 1974). On the other hand, beyond these norms, relatively little empirical information on the test is available. Before the primary study was undertaken, a side question was investigated: Is the CLEP Examination in General Psychology a valid and reliable measure of student achievement in psychology? Results of this aspect of the study indicated that the examination is psycho-

Table 4

Example of Judges' Descriptions of Project Advance and Syracuse University Papers Written at Level II

	Organization (Development and progression; consistency; agreement present and well done, paragraphing, transitions)	*Support* (Presence; type; sufficiency; appropriateness)
Project Advance Passing	Generally good organization (through the use of sophisticated modes of organization). Clear beginning, middle, and end. Clear sense of what an argument is. Arguments are convincing. Good progression across paragraphs and good transitions. Good and varied paragraphs, internally well organized.	Assertions almost always supported by a variety of types of support—authority, facts (some irrelevant), opinions, emotional appeal, etc. Support is generally sufficient and appropriate.
Project Advance Failing	Papers are organized (but the range is poor to good). Paragraphs are in the appropriate order, but the organization within paragraphs is often lacking. Transitions are recognized as important but not well handled.	Assertions generally supported by a number of pieces of evidence. Support is generally sufficient. Types of support include mostly facts (though they may be incorrect), opinion (but seldom used exclusively). Support is generally appropriate to assertion).
Syracuse University Passing	Major problems with organization. Development is weak or non-existent (often repeti-	Support is present but frequently insufficient. Evidence is often opinion and cliches.

tive); not clearly divided into parts. Little ordering between paragraphs. Transitions were inappropriate. Students seemed to have little or no grasp of the logical structure of what the argument should be like to convince the reader.

Syracuse University Failing

Organization was poor. Papers were serially ordered (series of unintegrated statements). Generally no beginning or end, or the end is "forced." There is a concept of "paragraphs," but it is weak (sometimes too much in a paragraph, sometimes too little in a paragraph). Little ordering within and between paragraphs. No transitions.

Some attempts at support; no formal distinctions between types of evidence. Restatement of assertions offered as support. More frequent use of unsupported opinion. Support is sometimes inappropriate, generally inadequate. Writers appear not to know how to support their assertions.

metrically sound, has respectable reliability (alpha = .83), and correlates moderately well with college students' grade in class (r = .61).

The results of the comparison of high school and college student performance indicated that the high school students who completed a college psychology course through P.A. scored significantly lower on the CLEP examination than did the college students as a whole but the same as college students on the Syracuse campus. Of more serious concern was the low correlation between CLEP scores and grades for the SUPA course (.30) compared to the college courses (.61). It appeared the differences are due to the problems in the point distribution for material in the SUPA course rather than to the high school students.

While the study had several purposes, one of the most valuable was the external validation of the course. Previously, the course stood up well under logical analysis and it was traditional in most respects in content, scope, and sequences. Additionally, students previously completing the course had scored significantly higher on course-specific tasks than had students completing other introductory psychology courses. The low correlation of grades to scores was a surprise and a disappointment and required immediate changes in course design. The experience was necessary, however, since only through public and objective assessment can the quality of such course offerings be verified.

Is the college credit students earn easily transferable to other colleges and universities?

The transferability of the college credit is regarded by many students as the single most important criterion of a successful program. Indeed, many of the potential advantages of these programs to the student assume the willingness and ability of colleges to accept the college credit generated by these programs.

If students earn college credit but cannot transfer it to the college of their choice, it does them little good as college credit and eventually undermines student confidence in the program. Unfortunately, programs frequently lack information on the experience of their students. While many colleges and universities across the country are presently involved in some form of high school cooperation, these programs have often emerged as local initiatives and served a primarily local clientele. Few locally based programs have had the resources to undertake

54

follow-up studies. Moreover, until recently, few programs made any claims that their credit was transferable beyond the sponsoring institution; transferability, then, was a peripheral concern.

One way to determine the transferability of credit is with a mailed questionnaire (sent to students after they have gone on to college) on which they are able to indicate the treatment their credit received. A sample questionnaire of this type of study is presented in the Appendix. A recent article (Wilbur & Chapman, 1977) describes how such a study was designed and conducted.

*What is the impact of the program on the
sponsoring institution?*

The motives for sponsoring an articulation program vary widely. Even when the incentives are primarily educational and emerge from a genuine interest in expanding opportunities for students, it is not unreasonable that a college realize some return. Likewise, the value of a program is seldom so self-evident as not to warrant periodic reassessment. Indeed, during this time of declining resources in higher education, a program that only "breaks even" may be held in suspicion by the larger institution. Moreover, the power and the presence of persons concerned with these outcomes are keenly felt by program administrators.

It is important, then, that programs keep good records on institutional impact. The consideration must go beyond just the profit-loss statement or number of high school students attracted to the sponsoring institution; it must consider the impact of the program on the academic quality of the students and their retention at the institution.

For example, a study of the enrollment and attrition of Project Advance students coming to Syracuse University showed that the number of students applying was about what it had always been from those high schools. However, a more careful analysis showed that of those accepted a larger percentage actually came. The financial advantage was not initial applications, but eventual yield. Moreover, it appears that Project Advance students tend to have a lower dropout rate than Syracuse University students as a whole—again resulting in positive financial impact on the sponsoring institution.

College admissions offices typically keep records of applicants from each high school each year with their test scores and other pertinent information. The registrar usually has records of student attrition and reasons for attrition. However, the responsibility for keeping track of the particular enrollment and attrition figures for students entering from an articulation program usually rests with the program administrator unless special arrangements can be worked out.

What is the long-term impact of the articulation program on high school student's eventual college experience?

We often laud these programs for their impact on the students' college experience—to shorten it, enrich it, or both. But we often forget to check. Did students who took an introductory college course in high school do well in the next course in that area when they went to college? Was their college course in high school good preparation? What do students themselves say about their articulation program after they have gone on to college and are looking back?

The unsolicited comments you may receive will tend to be from unhappy students who have a bone to pick, or from overjoyed students who just want you to know. But what is the typical experience? To know that, you probably have to ask. A follow-up study of Project Advance students who had gone on to college revealed that they had indeed done well academically, but what they valued most was that they had learned survival skills needed in college. Their experience with a Project Advance course in high school had taught them how to organize and manage their time, and it had taught them how to study.

Are the instructional materials used in the course effective? Does their use in the course facilitate learning?

In considering a new course, most attention focuses on cost and usability. Teachers and school administrators often do not ask for evidence that course materials are instructionally effective; i.e., that they produce desired learning outcomes. Yet this is an essential element of successful teaching and learning. Often the quality of the material is assumed, perhaps because of the eminence of the author or because, "It's the same material we use on campus." It may be the same material used on campus, but that by itself is not evidence of its effectiveness.

The sponsors of a school-college program should be able to answer the following questions about their course materials: Do they cover the content they are supposed to cover? This question might be answered through a content analysis showing that the issues and concepts covered in the material are similar to those covered in other materials purporting to teach the same or similar content. Do students know more after using the materials than they did before using them? This may be determined by testing students before and after they have used the materials. Another concern, closely related to the issue of effective material, is the appropriateness of the materials within the course. Are they introduced at the right times? Are directions for their use clear? Is the material correctly targeted and paced? Overlooking these questions can cause frustration and lack of interest in students and teachers alike.

Most often these questions are best answered by the students and teachers actually using the materials. One way is to ask students to complete a brief "miniquest" (Figure 3), or a similar questionnaire, on which they rate the clarity, pacing, and sequencing of the material.

How effective is the teaching? What teacher behaviors and course characteristics contribute to desired outcomes of the program?

While many school-college programs are employing PSI or audiotutorial teaching techniques and a few are using newer experimental techniques, most still rely on an instructor to present the material or at least to mediate the learning activities. Teachers want to know that their teaching activities have impact on student learning. Likewise, the institution sponsoring a course has a duty to provide optimal conditions for success for both teachers and students. However, this whole issue has often been a deep source of frustration. The activities that describe effective teaching are many and complex. Few school-college programs have any strategy for monitoring the effectiveness of instructors' teaching beyond an occasional super-

Figure 3

Miniquest

Student Evaluation of Materials

Date _____ Material Title _____
Course Title _____ Instructor _____

Please circle the most appropriate alternative.

1. This sequence of material was:
   (1) extremely interesting
   (2) interesting
   (3) somewhat interesting
   (4) uninteresting
   (5) boring

2. The material was paced:
   (1) much too fast
   (2) a little too fast
   (3) just right
   (4) a little too slow
   (5) much too slow

3. I learned:
   (1) a great deal
   (2) some
   (3) not very much
   (4) nothing

4. This sequence was:
   (1) very clear
   (2) clear
   (3) slightly confusing
   (4) very confusing

5. What I learned was:
   (1) very important
   (2) important
   (3) generally unimportant
   (4) a waste

6. Generally, this sequence was:
   (1) excellent
   (2) good
   (3) fair
   (4) poor

7. Please write at least one specific comment here. Thank you.

Please indicate any questions raised by the sequence.

MINI-QUEST © Center for Instructional Development, Syracuse University, 1972

58

visory visit during a class period.

Many colleges and some high schools have tried to respond to this concern by collecting student ratings of instruction. But these data are often tied more closely to faculty advancement than to course improvement. The statements students rate are more often global expressions of effectiveness—

- Overall, this teacher was (excellent/good/fair/poor)

rather than specific descriptions of course related activities—

- This teacher gives big assignments on short notice. (strongly agree / agree / undecided / disagree / strongly disagree).

The problem, then, is that information collected on global rating forms may not be specific enough to suggest a means of improvement.

One recent response to this problem is the Classroom Behavioral Survey, or CBS (Chapman, Holloway, & Kelly, 1978; Kelly & Chapman, 1977). The CBS consists of 66 statements which form eight subscales representing major aspects of classroom activity and teacher behavior identified in previous literature on student ratings (Rosenshine & Furst, 1971). These include the following:

1. Business-like behavior of the teacher
2. Teacher clarity
3. Difficulty
4. Practical value of the course
5. Teacher enthusiasm
6. Excitement
7. Dullness
8. Opportunity to practice criterion behavior.

Project Advance offers one example of its use. At the end of each semester, students in every classroom complete the CBS on machine-scorable answer sheets. Each teacher receives a summary of his or her students' responses and those of all students combined. The items are specific enough to suggest ways to improve in weak areas. For example, if a teacher receives a low rating in "teacher clarity," the teacher can respond to that issue by:

1. Using more examples to illustrate ideas;

2. Using fewer words that students are not likely to know; and/or
3. Asking students to comment on what is happening in class, etc.

In addition to reporting this information directly to teachers, it can be used in a program of research to provide future teachers in the program with a description of what works and what doesn't. For example, Project Advance found that students' perceptions of their teacher's enthusiasm was a significant predictor of student achievement in a PSI psychology course (Chapman, Holloway, & Kelly, 1978). The impact and influence of the instructor cannot be assumed nor can it be overlooked in designing a school-college program—regardless of whether those instructors are college teachers at a nearby university or high school teachers teaching in their own classroom. Examples of statements used in a recent form of the Classroom Behavioral Survey appear in the Appendix.

Which students are most likely to earn college credit?

Before students enroll in a college credit course, they frequently want to be assured that they "have what it takes" to do the work and earn the credit. Teachers and guidance counselors also want a set of standards they can use in student advising. Many articulation programs, on the other hand, are reluctant or unable to provide this type of information. For one thing, good predictive measures are few, and it would be unfair to the student to rely on a selection measure with marginal reliability or validity. But equally important, college credit courses in the high school are often an opportunity for students to "try out" college-level work. These programs may provide academically average students with a testing ground for their interests and abilities. Motivation may well be a more important factor than aptitude in a student's eventual success.

Yet there is still a need for good advising. Perhaps description is more likely to be valuable than prediction. Through careful thought and systematic data collection, a program can develop a composite description of students who have succeeded and those who have not. This description might include previous grade point average, test scores, and personal demographic data. Students wondering if they can "make it" have something to compare themselves against—a description of the academic and personal characteristics of those who have gone before.

What is the long-term impact of the program on the high school curriculum?

As high school-college programs have developed, most attention has been directed to the academic outcomes accruing to the individual student or the benefits to the sponsoring institution. Little, if any, attention, has been given to the impact of these programs on the curricula of the participating schools. Yet it seems reasonable to expect that the instruction of college courses would have some far-reaching impact on the high school program. High school personnel are concerned and under considerable pressure to ensure that their college-bound students can do college-level work. Participation in a college program serves to clarify the demands and the standards of college work. This, in turn, may have repercussions on the earlier preparation of students who enrolled in these courses.

One example of impact on the high school curricula is the freshman English course offered through Project Advance. Evidence of the course's impact on the high school curricula comes primarily in three ways: the school visits by P.A. staff and faculty, the one-day teacher seminars held each semester, and the fall report submitted by each teacher each year.

SUPA English has had a demonstrable influence on the high school English program in 18 of the 45 schools in which it is currently offered. However, two of those schools are offering it for the first time. Its influence is more realistically stated as 18 out of 43 schools. In examining those 18 cases, three patterns or levels of influence can be discerned:

1. The operation of SUPA English has led high schools to re-examine their English elective program as a preparation for college composition. Specifically, it has led some schools to identify, early in the tenth year, students likely to benefit from a college experience during their senior year and direct them through an "appropriate" prerequisite program (five schools).

2. Several schools have introduced structured composition

61

beginning at grade 10 as a means of strengthening the entire composition sequence (nine schools).

3. Dissatisfaction with student preparation for SUPA English has led some schools to redesign the entire English curriculum along lines suggested by the apparent strengths of the SUPA course (four schools).

Why should a single college course offered often to only a handful of students in each school have this kind of influence on so many high school programs? It might reasonably be understood as a fortunate accident of history. The impact of the SUPA English course was heavily influenced by the social and political context in which it was introduced. It came to the attention of the schools at a time when they were faced with increasing demands for accountability, public criticism of more imaginative humanities-inspired elective programs, a decline in SAT scores, and a widespread feeling that the schools should go "back to basics." Its design, its content, and its vocabulary provided tools which schools could use in responding to these other problems.

As teachers came under fire, the publicly defined criteria of the SUPA English course provided teachers and school administrators with a language and a conceptual framework for talking about good writing, and tangibly related those criteria to college credit for work in a college course. The willingness of the university to state the components of good college writing provided a language and a legitimacy to high schools trying to describe and defend the components of their own program.

One area of concern, then, in the evaluation of a high school-college program is the impact of that program on the high school curriculum. In addition to the example provided by SUPA English, where a college program "legitimized" and provided a language for curricular changes, a program might influence a school curriculum through its inservice training of high school teachers. The impact of articulation programs on the schools is an important factor in the long-term durability of the school-college cooperative movement.

4. Questions You Should Ask Any College or University Wanting To Work with Your School

THE GROWING NUMBER OF programs offering high school students an opportunity to earn college credit has given many schools some choice in selecting programs best suited to their students and their school district. The differences in programs can be important even when they are subtle. Such variations, for example, may involve costs to students and schools, required facilities, transferability of credit, and location of instruction. What follows is a series of questions that can clarify the distinctions among programs and help array information that school personnel may need to make decisions. The list is not exhaustive; it is intended only to suggest areas of concern. We expect that you will expand the list to meet your own specific requirements.

1. What type of student is the program designed to serve?
   - Primarily the academically gifted?
   - A broad range of college-bound students?
   - Open enrollment of students?

2. Who is to do the teaching?
   - High school faculty?
   - College faculty?
   - Teaching teams of college and high school faculty?

3. Where is the instruction to take place?
   - In the high school?
   - On the college campus?
   - At a combination of high school and college facilities?

4. What types of courses are offered?
   - General education (e.g., English composition, calculus, biology?
   - Elective (e.g., psychology, sociology)?
   - Professional (e.g., communications, brass instruments)?

5. Are there good predictors of student performance in the course?
   - Has research shown certain factors to correlate with success in the program or in particular courses (e.g., reading ability, previous related course work)?

- Are there recommended procedures for student advisers?

6. Is the participating district committed to a specified number of courses or students?
    - Can schools add or drop courses or expand or reduce enrollment as interest and other factors dictate?
    - What procedures and resources are used for expansion and reduction?
    - What financial obligations are involved?

7. Are standards of performance for each course in the program clearly established?
    - Are these criteria easily understood by students and teachers?
    - Have course manuals for students and teachers been developed?
    - Are these standards generally in line with those of other colleges and universities?

8. Have the instructional materials been validated?
    - Do they present content widely regarded as appropriate to the course?
    - Are the materials effective in communicating the content?
    - Has the course material been developed through a systematic process?

9. Does the program regularly undergo systematic evaluation?
    - What kinds of questions are asked?
    - Have adequate resources been provided for the evaluation?
    - Is there an opportunity for school officials to request that additional questions be added?
    - How are evaluation data processed? To whom are they made available? What use is made of the data?

10. Is a particular pedagogy or teaching strategy employed?
    - Does it use, for example, the Keller system or audio-tutorial methods?
    - How does the design of the course affect the teacher's role?
    - Are special facilities required?

11. What are the costs of the program to students and the school district?
    - What does it cost the district to implement the program (e.g., instructional materials, teacher training, travel of teachers)?
    - What are the maintenance expenses (e.g., instructional material replacements, substitute costs while teachers attend periodic seminars)?
    - What, if any, costs fall to the students who participate (e.g., tuition for college registration, instructional materials, transcript fee)?

12. What are the criteria for teacher selection (in programs where a high school teacher has the primary responsibility for the instruction)?
    - What kind of teaching experience or academic preparation is required?
    - What is the school's role in selecting or nominating teachers?

13. Are there established procedures for preparing high school faculty to teach in the program?
    - Are these formal or informal?
    - Do they involve out-of-school time for the teachers?
    - What are the costs to the school district?

14. Are there provisions for students to earn high school as well as college credit for work completed in the program?
    - If so, are there separate grading systems?
    - May students enroll only for high school credit without paying tuition?

15. How widely transferable is the credit students earn?
    - Is a regular transcript issued by the sponsoring institution?
    - Has the transferability been thoroughly documented?
    - Does the sponsoring institution have staff responsible for helping students explain the program and credits to officials at other institutions?

16. What is the relationship of the high school faculty (in cases where they are teaching the college courses) to the academic departments at the sponsoring institution?

Table 5

Sample Chart for Comparing Features of Two or More School-College Cooperative Programs

Question	Program A	Program B	Program C
1. Students served?	Top and average college-bound students with minimum verbal and math SAT's usually in lower to mid-500's.	Top academic group; top 6-10% of SAT scores for college-bound students nationally	Top and average college-bound students. No data regarding typical SAT scores of participants.
2. Location of instruction?	High school	High school	High school
3. Courses offered?	Freshman English, biology, calculus, chemistry, psychology, sociology	Wide selection of general education and elective course	American history, calculus, and sociology
11. Costs to student? district?	$17 per credit hour $450 for initial teacher training; $20-30/student for initial instructional materials; $5-15 for re-placement of expendables; costs of occasional substitutes for semi-annual faculty seminars; possible teacher load adjustments	$28 examination fee $20-30/student for initial instructional materials; $5-10 for replacement of expendables	$67 per credit hour $20-30/student for initial instructional materials; $5-15 for replacement of expendables

12. Teacher selection?	High school nominates interested teachers who have academic and teaching background specified by university. Approval by committee of university faculty.	Selection made by high school.	None. Instructors from university teach course in the high school.
13. Teacher training?	Formal two-week workshops and continuing semi-annual seminar series.	Occasional workshops available. None necessary.	None.

- Do they hold academic appointment?
- Is this appointment subject to periodic review?
- Are there continuing requirements which the teacher must fulfill to retain the appointment (e.g., attendance at seminars, filing annual written reports)?
- What are the responsibilities of the high school and the sponsoring institution in maintaining academic standards?

17. Have all legal and procedural problems with the program been satisfactorily resolved?
    - Have they been reviewed by appropriate state education department agencies?
    - Are there approved methods for handling tuition or instructional materials monies?

18. Has a solid administrative structure been established by the sponsoring institution to ensure delivery of quality services and, to the extent possible, longevity of the program?
    - Does the staff have the needed interest and experience to do this?
    - Are the participating college teachers stable in their positions and interested in a long-term relationship with secondary school students and teachers?
    - Are procedures regarding registration, transfer of credits, site visits, and faculty training sessions clear?
    - Are the obligations and responsibilities of both the school and sponsoring institution thoughtfully delineated?

The preceding questions should help you begin to establish your own criteria for judging an established or developing a school-college cooperative program. We encourage you to incorporate liberally other questions raised by members of your faculty, school board, and community. *You* must decide what features are most important or least desirable for your district.

Table 5 suggests a way to compare two or more programs that may be available to your district.

In evaluating programs, think in terms of the long-range benefits and problems; remember, adoption is usually the easiest part of the process. A hastily conceived and casually administered program will probably fail to produce the desired results for the district or the college. Many school administrators are interested not only in the opportunity for their students to earn credit in representative college courses but also in such outcomes as promoting the continued professional growth of their staff through the college affiliation, sharing educational resources with area colleges and universities, and improving the ability of the high school to respond to the changing needs of students. It may also be useful to contact school administrators and college officials in other areas of the country that have had experience in dealing with questions that seem particularly crucial. (See the Appendix for a list of contacts throughout the country.)

5. Summary and Conclusions

In CHAPTER ONE WE began our discussion of cooperative programing by briefly reviewing the history of poor curriculum coordination between high schools and colleges, and then considered the educational problems caused by this discontinuity. Most of these problems have been recognized for some time. However, their intensification in the past decade has led some institutions to try to resolve them by developing new cooperative programs or by finding new applications for old programs. Chapter One concluded with a brief consideration of four workable models of school-college cooperative programs, their characteristic advantages and disadvantages.

In Chapter Two we dealt with a more difficult aspect of our subject—how to implement a cooperative program. The blueprint presented related to a specific articulation program—Syracuse University Project Advance. We chose a specific program not only because it is easier to illustrate general statements with specific examples, but also because we wanted to describe more than just a theoretical model. Theoretical models are notoriously free of difficulties that are inescapable when the ideal becomes actual; they are too good to be true. We selected a model that has imperfections and that has undergone almost continuous change in responding to problems, confident that administrators and principals would rather be guided by a scout who candidly tells them about the dangers in the wilderness as well as the treasures to be found there. The difficulties of implementation include financing, staffing, and administration.

Consequently, we explained how to fund an articulation program, what incentives there were for high school and college faculty to collaborate, how to define responsibilities and roles, what problems to anticipate, and how to resolve them.

Chapter Three dealt with the important role of evaluation in a cooperative program. It discussed the kinds of evaluation activities that must be built into an articulation program to address characteristic concerns of parents, students, and college officials. Evaluation, like medical diagnosis, tells us when the organizational body is healthy and when it is sick; how it can be kept well, and how it can be made well.

In Chapter Four we offered guidelines in the form of questions for judging the quality of existing or proposed articulation programs. The questions represent an efficient way to assess a cooperative program and are the fruit of our own experience.

The first four chapters of this monograph have tried to answer the why, how, and what of cooperative programs, but it is impossible to discuss in detail every problem that may arise. We therefore recommend to the reader that he consult the references listed at the end of the monograph for further information. The reader may also find it helpful to refer to the directory of some of the high schools that have been involved in cooperative college programs (see Appendix). Compiled by NASSP in the summer of 1977, the list provides the name and address of each high school principal, indicates the courses offered in each location, and identifies the affiliated college or university. Although far from comprehensive, the list provides a good selection of programs by type, size, and location of high school and content areas. The administrators at these schools should be able to answer questions about the programs and offer views from a different perspective.

In high school-college cooperative programs the key word is "cooperative." If people in both institutions are not willing to work together, drawing on a reservoir of mutual trust and respect, joint programing will not work. The difficulties in such a venture, particularly in a SUPA-type program, are so numerous and the structure so inherently fragile that, if there is not a strong commitment on both sides, the venture will probably fail from the beginning or collapse when the first serious problem arises. For problems will arise. There is no way to ensure trouble-free experience; all that can be done is to plan carefully and be prepared to meet trouble courageously.

In addition to the specific problems discussed in this monograph, there are general problems that attend any significant change. There will be resistance from people afraid to part with the familiar, from people unconvinced that change will mean needed improvement, or from people who may feel threatened politically or economically. All of these suggest the importance of proper deliberation before embarking on so complicated an enterprise.

But despite the difficulties encountered, we have found the cooperative venture to be well worth the cost. In addition to the benefits originally anticipated and which were the chief motives for establishing joint programing, we discovered other benefits that we had not expected. Working with high school teachers and administrators and with enthusiastic high school seniors has been not only enjoyable but educational as well.

When SUPA first began, for example, some campus faculty members expressed misgivings about the capacity of high school instructors to teach the courses and of high school seniors to handle them. The first year of the program quickly dispelled these fears. In fact, in at least one university department several changes in the on-campus course structure were made as a result of improvements manifest in the high schools.

Articulation, in other words, was seen by many as an opportunity for the university to influence the high school curriculum. This did happen, especially in high schools that adjusted the earlier high school years to accommodate college expectations seen close up. The opposite also happened as the high schools influenced the university curriculum.

SUPA students also discovered advantages to the program they had not entirely expected. Participation in the program enabled them to develop academic survival skills which were extremely useful to them later when they went off to college.

Our experience with joint programing has also demonstrated that it is possible for traditionally disparate school systems to collaborate, even on a large scale. This alone is valuable knowledge. Perhaps the most urgent need now for cooperative programing is to have those groups around the country currently working in isolation get together at national and regional meetings or institutes to exchange information and ideas. Additional documentation of cooperative programs and greater publicity should enhance public understanding and facilitate program dissemination. Here strong support from state education departments, national organizations, and foundations would do much to assist high school-college articulation.

At the same time, we must remember that there is a Gresham's Law of Education: poor cooperative programs can drive good cooperative programs out of circulation. This highlights the need for standards to ensure that articulation programs maintain academic excellence. As the knowledge spreads that it is possible to have cooperative programing consistent with the highest standards of academic excellence, unthinking opposition, particularly from institutions which automatically or capriciously withhold recognition of college credit earned through non-traditional programs, will diminish.

This monograph has been written primarily to serve these needs—to apprise high school and college administrators (the necessary catalysts of educational change) of new educational opportunities for high school students so that they may make informed choices in establishing or joining a high school-college cooperative program.

Appendix

Directory of Schools Cooperatively Sponsoring Programs with Colleges and Universities

The list below was compiled by the research and evaluation staff of NASSP during the summer of 1977. It is not meant to be exhaustive, but rather a first attempt to provide you with contacts at high schools with cooperative college programs in different parts of the country. In each case, the courses are offered in the high school building.

We request your assistance in updating and expanding this list. Please write to the Research Office, NASSP, 1904 Association Drive, Reston, Va. 22091, to inform us of cooperative programs in your area.

High School (Principal) Address and Telephone	College Courses Offered	Affiliated College(s) or University(ies)
Ballard Memorial (Chester Anderson) Route 1 Barlow, Ky. 42024 502-655-5151	Political science Philosophy	Paducah Community College
Bishop Kearney High School (Sister John Crucis) 60th St. & Bay Parkway Brooklyn, N.Y. 11204 212-837-6005	Health Religion Physical education English History	St. Joseph's College
Cambridge-South Dorchester High School (Ms. Walter) Maple Dam Road Cambridge, Md. 21613 301-228-9224	College biology Western civilization Calculus English	Salisbury State College
Colonial Central High School (Dr. Peruzzi) 100 Hackett Ave. Albany, N.Y. 518-459-1220	English History Advanced psychology Advanced sociology	Sienna State University Syracuse University

Fairport High School (Mr. Lyman C. Cook) 1358 Ayrault Rd. Fairport, N.Y. 14450 716-223-5858	English Chemistry Math Three foreign language courses	Nazareth College of Rochester

Wm. H. Hall High School
(Dr. Robert E. Dunn)
975 West Main Street
West Hartford, Conn.
  06117
203-232-4561
	*	University of Hartford
		Central Conn. State
		Hartford College for
		   Women

Hauppauge High School
(Richard N. Suprina)
Lincoln Blvd.
Hauppauge, N.Y. 11787
516-265-3630
	Calculus
	Principles of biology
	Zoology
	College accounting
	Advanced Spanish
	Advanced French
	College freshman
	  English
	English comic vision
	  literature
	English tragic vision
	  literature
	Religions of the world
	College psychology
		Syracuse University
		C. W. Post College
		Adelphi University
		Dowling College

Hayden High School (Thomas Santa) 401 Gage Street Topeka, Kans. 66606 913-272-5210	English composition Western civilization	St. Mary College Benedictine College

Lindbergh Sr. High
  School
(LeRoy Amen)
4900 South Lindbergh
  Blvd.
St. Louis, Mo. 63126
314-849-2000
	Calculus
	English composition
	American history
	Four foreign
	   language courses
		St. Louis University
		University of Missouri

Course offerings change yearly or information was not provided on survey instrument.

Liverpool High School
(David Kidd)
Wetzel Road
Liverpool, N.Y.
315-652-1300
	Biology
	English
	Psychology
	Calculus
	The era of the
	  American Revolu-
	  tion, 1689-1789
	North America Indian
	  history
	Sociology
	French
	Spanish
	Marketing
		Syracuse University
		SUNY—Oswego
		Adelphi University
		Onondaga Community
		  College

Manhasset High School (Warren McGregor) Manhasset, N.Y. 11030 516-627-4400	English composition Biology Calculus Psychology Sociology	Syracuse University
Plattsmouth High School (John J. Beck, Jr.) Plattsmouth, Nebr. 68048 402-296-3322	English literature and composition Introductory math Calculus Biology	Peru State College
Poca High School (Harold Carr) Poca, W.Va. 304-755-5001	Freshman English	West Virginia State College
Providence High School (Robert Larkin) 707 West Highway 131 Clarksville, Ind. 47130 812-945-2538	English composition English literature Psychology Sociology	Indiana University— Southeast
Roy High School (Darrell K. White) 2150 West 4800 South Roy, Utah 84067 801-825-9766	*	Weber State College University of Utah
Saint Scholastica Academy (Karen Blund) 615 Pike Street Canon City, Colo. 81212 303-275-7461	Science Spanish Mathematics	University of Colorado

*Course offerings change yearly or information was not provided on survey instrument.

Shaker High School   *
(Arthur E. Walker)
445 Shaker Road
Latham, N.Y. 12110
518-785-5511

SUNY—Plattsburgh
SUNY—Brockport
SUNY—Fredonia
SUNY—Geneseo
Hudson Valley
    Community College

Swarthmore High School
(Mr. Lichtenstein)
Swarthmore, Pa. 19081
215-544-5700

Calculus
American studies
French seminar

Widener College

Tupper Lake High School
(James Ellis)
Tupper Lake, N.Y. 12986
518-359-3322

English
Biology
Economics
Sociology

North Country
    Community College

Course offerings change yearly or information was not provided on survey instrument.

78

Sample Credit Transfer Survey Instruments

SYRACUSE UNIVERSITY CENTER FOR INSTRUCTIONAL
DEVELOPMENT
Project Advance

Questionnaire completed by:

Part A: This section of the questionnaire to be completed only by students who have *not yet* transferred their SUPA credit to a college or university.

1. Are you now attending a college, university, or professional school?

   ☐ yes   ☐ no

   If yes, please indicate the following:

   Name of college, university or school _____

   Address _____

          street   city   state   zip code

   If no, do you plan to attend college within the next 3 years?

   ☐ yes   ☐ no

2. If you enrolled at a college or university and decided not to transfer Project Advance credit, please indicate why not.

   ☐ My grade(s) in Project Advance were too low to transfer.

   ☐ College said they would not accept the credit so I didn't bother to request credit transfer.

   ☐ I decided that I would benefit by repeating a similar college course(s) as a college freshman.

   ☐ I didn't know that I was supposed to request an official Syracuse University transcript.

   ☐ Other (Explain) _____

   _____

3. If you found that Syracuse University Project Advance credit was not acceptable at another institution, how did you discover this?

   ☐ college catalog

   ☐ visit to institution

   ☐ letter from institution

   ☐ speaking with institutional representative
   (indicate the office or individual below)

       ☐ admissions office

       ☐ registrar's office

       ☐ advisor

☐ dean's office
☐ academic department
☐ other (e.g., student, college-night representative) _____

4. Please feel free to add additional comments that will help us understand problems you may have encountered in transferring or attempting to transfer Project Advance credit.

    Return this questionnaire in the pre-stamped envelope provided.

Part B: This section is to be completed only by students who *have* transferred SUPA credit to a college or university.

    Please check the appropriate box or supply the requested information.

5. College major or area of concentration _____
    ☐ check if not yet selected

6. What degree are you working toward? (Check one)
    ☐ Associate   ☐ Bachelor's   ☐ other _____

7. When did you ask your college to make a decision about your Syracuse University Project Advance credit?
    ☐ Before Accep-   ☐ After Accep-   ☐ After Accep-
       tance—Prior to   tance—Prior to   tance—After
       Registration   Campus   Campus
                               Registration   Registration

8. When were you informed, at least tentatively, as to your college's or university's decision regarding recognition of your Syracuse University Project Advance credit?
    ☐ Before Accep-   ☐ After Accep—   ☐ After Accep-
       tance—Prior to   tance—Prior to   tance— After
       Registration   Campus   Campus
                               Registration   Registration

9. Does your college or university have written policy related to their recognition of credit earned at other colleges by their entering freshmen?   ☐ yes   ☐ no   ☐ don't know

10. Who informed you of the decision made at your college or university regarding credit earned in Syracuse University Project Advance?
    ☐ Advisor   ☐ Admissions Office
    ☐ College Dean   ☐ Registrar's Office
    ☐ Department Chairman   ☐ Other (specify) _____

11. Were you told that your choice of major or area of concentration affected the number of Syracuse University Project Advance credits recognized at your college or university?

☐ yes   ☐ no

12. What information, in addition to the college transcript, did your college request before making a decision on the recognition of your Syracuse University Project Advance credit?

☐ Check here if you are not aware of any.

_____

_____

13. Please feel free to add additional comments that will help us understand any problems you may have encountered in transferring Syracuse University Project Advance credit.

After finishing part B of the questionnaire, please complete your *Student Transcript Data Form* according to the accompanying directions. Return both the questionnaire and data form in the enclosed, pre-stamped envelope.

_____

PROJECT ADVANCE Student Transcript Data Form

Important: Please complete your enclosed Transcript Data Form using the following procedure:

In the section of the form labeled *Institutional Action,* check only *one* of the five columns for *each* of the course grades. Foundations of Human Behavior involves only one grade and the traditional 3 credits. Freshman English is a variable credit course involving up to six course grades. Please indicate to the best of your knowledge what action the college or university you are now attending has taken for each course grade.

1. *Credit Only.* Check here if you received credit toward your degree requirements, but not exemption from a similar required course.

2. *Exemption Only.* Check here if you received exemption from a requirement in your degree program but received no credit. If you received an exemption but were told that credit will be deferred until after completion of an advanced course, also check this column and make a note on the back of your data form to this effect.

3. *Credit and Exemption.* Check if both were given.

4. *Neither Credit nor Exemption.* Check if neither was given.

5. *Other Action.* If you check this column, please give a brief ex-

planation on the back of your data form, i.e., "granting of credit or course exemption is against college policy," or "special degree requirements," etc.

6. *Number of Credits Accepted.* In this column, indicate the number of credits accepted by your college or university for each course or, in the case of English, each portion of the course. At the bottom of this column, indicate the total number of credits accepted.

7. We ask that you respond as soon as possible and forward both the questionnaire (Part A) and your transcript data form (Part B) in the return envelope provided.

Thank you again for your time and assistance.

Forward to: Franklin P. Wilbur
Associate in Development
Project Advance
759 Ostrom Avenue
Syracuse, New York 13210

PROJECT ADVANCE

(To be completed if credit transfer was requested)
Student Transcript Data Record Form S-1A (1975)

1. Please indicate the high school you attended last year and the college or university that you are now attending which has evaluated your SUPA transcript:

High School _____

College/University _____

Address of College _____
　　　　　　　　　　　　　street　　　　　　　　　　　　　　　　　city

_____
　　　　　　　　　　　state　　　　　　　　　　　　　　　　zip code

2. In the spaces provided, please indicate how your SUPA credit was recognized by the college you are now attending. Be sure to follow the instructions given on the previous page.

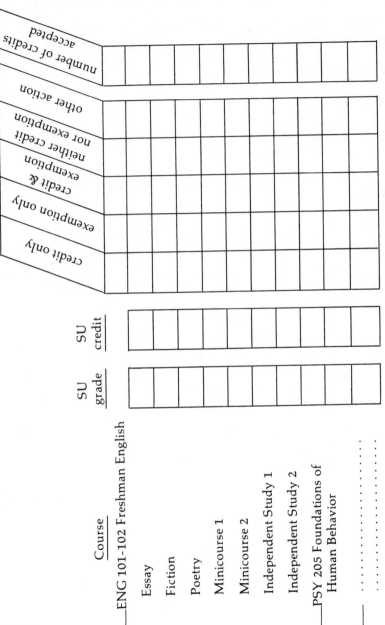

Course	SU grade	SU credit	credit only	exemption only	credit & exemption	neither credit nor exemption	other action	number of credits accepted
ENG 101-102 Freshman English								
Essay								
Fiction								
Poetry								
Minicourse 1								
Minicourse 2								
Independent Study 1								
Independent Study 2								
PSY 205 Foundations of Human Behavior								
....								
....								

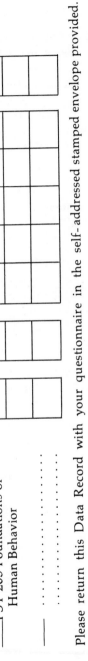

Please return this Data Record with your questionnaire in the self-addressed stamped envelope provided.

Examples of Questions Used on the Project Advance Course Evaluation (PACE) Form (1976 revised edition)

The following statements may describe your class and teacher. Please mark the appropriate place on your answer sheet to indicate how well you think each statement describes your classroom according to the following scale:

(A) Strongly Agree
(B) Agree
(C) Undecided
(D) Disagree
(E) Strongly Disagree

Do not skip any of the items. It is important that you respond to every statement.

1. This teacher explains complicated ideas and relationships clearly.
2. In this class we never cover all the materials we are supposed to.
3. Compared to other classes I've been in, this one deals with very complicated ideas.
4. I have trouble seeing how this class relates to other things I am studying.
5. This teacher enjoys teaching.
6. This teacher asks questions that really make me think.
7. In this class we cover the same material over and over again.
8. When this class period ends, I usually know that the most important material has been covered.
9. I frequently don't understand what's being discussed in class.
10. In this class it is hard to get your homework done by the time it is due.
11. This class has very little to do with anything that's important to know.
12. The course materials provide good practice exercises for the things I am tested on.
13. I would like to take more courses designed like this one.
14. This teacher speaks in a monotone.
15. Several of my best friends are in this class.
16. This teacher never knows when to stop answering a question.
17. In this classroom I am given a chance to learn things before I am tested on them.
18. Generally, this class bores me stiff.
19. In this class I usually understand why I get the grades I do.

20. I feel as if I am competing against the other students in this class.

21. In this class we learn things that are very practical.

22. This teacher frequently embarrasses students who make mistakes.

23. I feel very free to express my opinions in this class.

24. I already know most of what is being taught in this class.

25. Generally, I feel that students in this class have a good relationship with each other.

26. In this course the tests and papers correspond well to the study materials.

27. When answering a question, this teacher gets right to the point.

28. This teacher gets confused explaining the subject matter.

29. This course is more demanding than other courses I would have taken if it were not available.

30. This course is giving me a good background in this subject.

31. This teacher makes me feel that I'm an important person.

32. This teacher doesn't really teach anything because of the way this course is set up.

33. The teacher doesn't involve the students in discussions.

34. In this class, discussions are sometimes so exciting that I am sorry they end.

35. There are so many different things going on that it is difficult for me to learn anything.

36. This teacher usually gives good examples to illustrate ideas.

37. If I miss this class, I really get behind.

38. I have used what I am learning in this course in others I am taking.

39. In this class I am encouraged to practice those things on which I am tested.

40. This teacher is enthusiastic about teaching.

41. The teacher reads to us out of the text.

42. This teacher brings all the materials needed to teach the class.

43. When I don't understand the reasons for my grades, I feel free to ask this teacher to discuss them with me.

44. This is a very dull class.

45. In this class, what I am tested on corresponds well to what I have had a chance to learn.

46. Although I understand what is being taught in this course, I frequently have trouble applying it.

47. This teacher gets excited when students give good answers or say important things.
48. In this class we always do the same things.
49. In this class, the textbooks mesh well with what is taught.
50. It is hard to follow what this teacher means when he is lecturing.
51. This course is difficult because what I am learning is highly theoretical.
52. This teacher is fun to listen to.
53. This teacher gives big assignments on short notice.
54. In this class, I only get one chance to learn something.
55. This teacher frequently asks other students to comment on what has happened.
56. I frequently do not understand the words this teacher uses.
57. In this class, books and materials are available when needed.
58. This teacher tells us what we are expected to learn.
59. Although it seems clear in class, when I get home this class is confusing.
60. This teacher tells us well in advance about changes in assignments and classes.
61. This teacher assumes things I don't know.
62. It is easy to follow this teacher's classroom presentation.
63. Frequently one or two students monopolize the class discussion.
64. This teacher is clear about what I am expected to learn.
65. This course is difficult because I have a hard time applying the concepts.
66. I frequently don't understand the textbook.

©*D. W. Chapman and E. F. Kelly, Center for Instructional Development, Syracuse University, 1976*

References

Blanchard, B. E. *A National Survey of Curriculum Articulation Between the College of Liberal Arts and the Secondary School.* Chicago: DePaul University Press, 1971.

Bowen, H. R. "Time, Informal Learning, and Efficiency in Higher Education." *Educational Record* 54 (1973): 271-281.

Bremer, J. W. *Advanced Placement Programs and Economics.* Fullerton: California State College, 1968. ERIC ED077783.

Brown, B. F. (chairman). *The Reform of Secondary Education: Report of the National Commission on the Reform of Secondary Education.* New York: McGraw-Hill, 1973.

Bruner, J. S. *The Process of Education.* New York: Vintage Books, 1960.

Carnegie Commission on Higher Education. *Continuity and Discontinuity: Higher Education and the Schools.* New York: McGraw-Hill, 1973.

Casserly, P. L. *College Decisions on Advanced Placement: A Follow-up of Advanced Placement Candidates of 1963.* Princeton, N.J.: Educational Testing Service, 1965.

Chapman, D.; Holloway, R.; and Kelly, E. "Using Ratings by Students to Predict High and Low Achievers in a P.S.I. Course: A Discriminant Analysis." *AV Communication Review*, Winter 1978.

College Entrance Examination Board. *A Guide to the Advanced Placement Program.* New York: College Entrance Examination Board, 1974.

Crowley, W. H. "A Ninety-Year-Old Conflict Erupts Again." *Educational Record*, January 1942, pp. 192-218.

DeVane, W. C. "A Time and Place for Liberal Education." *Liberal Education* 46 (1964): 467-483.

Diamond, R. M. "Syracuse University: A Systematic Approach to Curriculum and Faculty Development." In *New Directions for Higher Education.* No. 15, Autumn 1976. A Comprehensive Approach to Institutional Development, edited by W. H. Bergquist & W. A. Shoemaker. San Francisco: Jossey-Bass, Inc., 1976.

Eurich, A. C., and Scranton, J. J. "Articulation of Educational Units." In *Encyclopedia of Educational Research*, edited by C. W. Harris. New York: Macmillan Company, 1960.

Fleischmann Commission. *The Fleischmann Report on the Quality, Costs, and Financing of Elementary and Secondary Education in New York State.* Vol. 2. New York: Viking Press, 1973.

General Education in Schools and Colleges: A Committee Report. Cambridge, Mass.: Harvard University Press, 1952.

Gleazer, E. J., Jr. *A.A.C.J.C. Approach.* Washington, D.C.: American Association of Community and Junior Colleges, 1973.

Kelly, E., and Chapman, D. "Explaining Course Oriented Attitude." *Educational Research Quarterly,* Fall 1977.

Lindsay, F. D. "Advanced Placement Program." *California Education,* November 1965, pp. 7-11.

Magill, S. H. *Report on Time-Shortened Degree Programs.* Washington, D.C.: American Association of Community and Junior Colleges, 1973.

National Association of Secondary School Principals. "College Courses: A Twelfth Grade Option." *Curriculum Report,* December 1975.

Nelson, J. H. "New Challenges in Articulation." Speech presented at 39th annual meeting of the Upper Midwest Association of College Registrars and Admissions Officers, University of North Dakota, Grand Forks, October 23, 1972.

New York State Department of Education. "Going Non-Traditional: Crossing the High School-College Divide." *Inside Education,* July 1974, p. 7.

Osborn, W. J. *Overlapping and Omission in Our Course of Study.* Bloomington, Ill.: Public School Publishing Company, 1928.

Pincus, J. "Incentives for Innovation in the Public School." *Review of Educational Research* 44 (1974): 113-139.

Regents of the University of the State of New York. *The Articulation of Secondary and Postsecondary Education.* Position Paper No. 21. Albany: State Education Department, 1974.

Rosenshine, B., and Furst, N. "Research on Teacher Performance Criteria." In *Research in Teaching,* edited by D. O. Smith. Englewood Cliffs, N.J.: Prentice-Hall, 1971.

Russell, J. D. *The American Educational System.* Chicago: Houghton Mifflin Co., 1940.

Sizer, T. R. "When They Leave High School." *The Chronicle of Higher Education* 8 (1973): 5.

Snyder, N. "School-College Articulation and the Maginot Line." Speech delivered at the commissioner's Second Annual Conference on Non-traditional Studies, Glens Falls, New York, October, 2-4, 1975.

Tom, A. P. "Three Dilemmas: School-University Ventures." *The Clearing House,* September 1973, pp. 7-10.

Willingham, W. W. *College Placement and Exemption.* New York: College Entrance Examination Board, 1974.

Wilbur, F. *School-College Articulation: Cooperative Programs and Practices Linking Secondary and Post-Secondary Curricula.* Research Report #5, Center for Instructional Development, Syracuse University, 1975.

Wilbur, F., and Chapman, D. "The Transferability of College Credit Earned During High School." *College and University*, Spring 1977.

Selected Bibliography

Acceleration and Time-Shortened Degrees

Allen, E. L. "The Three-Year Baccalaureate." *The Journal of General Education*, April 1973, pp. 61-73.

Bersi, R. M. *Restructuring the Baccalaureate: A Focus on Time-Shortened Degrees in the United States*. Washington, D.C.: American Association of State Colleges and Universities, 1973.

Bish, C. F. "What Are the Advantages and Disadvantages of Acceleration?" In *Educating the Academically Able*, edited by L. D. Crow and A. Crow. New York: McKay, 1963.

Carnegie Commission on Higher Education. *Less Time, More Options: Education Beyond the High School*. New York: McGraw-Hill, 1971.

Conklin, K. R. "The Three-Year B.A.: Boon or Bust?" *AAUP Bulletin*, March 1972, pp. 35-39.

Frost, J. A. "Time-Shortening and Articulation." In *Higher Education: Myths, Realities, and Possibilities*, edited by W. L. Godwin and P. B. Mann. Atlanta, Ga.: South Regional Education Board, 1972.

Fund for the Advancement of Education. *They Went to College Early*. Evaluation Report Number 2. New York: Fund for the Advancement of Education, 1957.

Meinert, C. W. *Time Shortened Degrees*. Washington, D.C.: American Association for Higher Education, 1974.

Miller, J. W. *Male Student Success in the Collegiate Early Admission Experiment*. Honolulu: University of Hawaii Press, 1968. ERIC ED068017.

Pressey, S. L. *Educational Acceleration: Appraisals and Basic Problems*. Columbus: Ohio State University Press, 1949.

Radcliffe, S., and Hatch, W. R. *Advanced Standing*. Washington, D.C.: Office of Education, U.S. Department of Health, Education, and Welfare, 1961.

Stark, J. S. "The Three-Year B.A.: Who Will Choose It? Who Will Benefit?" *The Journal of Higher Education*, December 1973, pp. 703-715.

Van Gelder, E. "The Three-Year B.A.: A Wavering Idea." Gainesville, Fla.: Florida University, 1972. ERIC ED070434.

Non-Traditional Learning

Creager, J. A. *Selected Policies and Practices in Higher Education*. ACE Research Reports, Vol. 8, No. 4. Washington, D.C.: American Council on Education, 1973.

Current Practices in the Assessment of Experiential Learning. CAEL

Working Paper No. 1. Princeton, N.J.: Cooperative Assessment of Experiential Learning, September 1974.

Gould, S. D., ed. *Diversity by Design*. San Francisco: Jossey-Bass, 1973.

Nelson, F. A. "Has the Time Gone for an External Degree?" *Journal of Higher Education*, March 1974, pp. 174-183.

Ruyle, J., and Geiselman, L. A. Non-Traditional Opportunities and Programs." In *Planning Non-Traditional Programs: An Analysis of the Issues of Post-Secondary Education*, edited by K. P. Cross, J. R. Valley, and Associates. San Francisco: Jossey-Bass, 1974.

Trivett, D. A. *Academic Credit for Prior Off-Campus Learning*. Washington, D.C.: American Association for Higher Education, 1974.

Research on Innovation in Education

Carlson, R. O. *Adoption of Educational Innovations*. Eugene, Oreg.: University of Oregon, 1965.

Diamond, R. M.; Eickmann, P.; Kelly, E. F.; Holloway, R. E.; Vickery, T. R.; and Pascarella, E. T. *Instructional Development for Individualized Learning in Higher Education*. Englewood Cliffs, N.J.: Educational Technology Publications, 1975.

Havelock, R. G. *The Change Agent's Guide to Innovation in Education*. Englewood Cliffs, N.J.: Educational Technology Publications, 1973.

Pincus, J. "Incentives for Innovation in the Public School." *Review of Education Research*, 44 (1974): 113-139.

Rogers, M., and Shoemaker, F. F. *Communication of Innovations*. New York: The Free Press, 1971.

Background, Issues, and Research on
Secondary—Post-Secondary Articulation

Blocker, C. "Cooperation Between Two-Year and Four-Year Colleges." *School and Society* 94 (1966): 218-222. ERIC EJ016469.

Carnegie Commission on Higher Education. *A Chance To Learn: An Action Agenda for Equal Opportunity in Higher Education*. New York: McGraw-Hill, 1970.

Chapman, D., and Wilbur, F. "Project Advance—College Courses in the High School Classroom." *New York State Personnel and Guidance Journal* 11 (1976): 1.

Diamond, R. M., and Holloway, R. *Project Advance: An Alternative Approach to High School-College Articulation*. Research Report #3. Syracuse, N.Y.: Center for Instructional Development, Syracuse University, 1975.

Elliott, L. "An Idea Whose Time Has Come." *Trends and Issues in Cooperation.* Washington, D.C.: American Association for Higher Education, 1973.

Gaines, B. C., and Chapman, D. "The Impact of College Courses in the High School on the High School Curricula." In *Research Report #12.* Syracuse, N.Y.: Center for Instructional Development, Syracuse University, 1977.

Holloway, R. "Perceptions of an Innovation: Syracuse University Project Advance." Doctoral dissertation, Syracuse University, Syracuse, N.Y., July 1977.

Kintzer, F. C. *Middleman in Higher Education: Improving Articulation Among High School, Community College, and Senior Institutions.* San Francisco: Jossey-Bass, 1973.

Kintzer, F. C. *Nationwide Pilot Study on Articulation.* Los Angeles: ERIC Clearinghouse for Junior Colleges, University of California, 1970.

National Association of Secondary School Principals. "College Courses: A Twelfth Grade Option." *Curriculum Report* 5 (1975): 2.

New York State Department of Education. "Linking Schools and Colleges: An Inventory of Articulation Practices in New York State." Albany, N.Y.: NYSDE, 1975.

Oregon High School-College Relations Council. *Guidelines for School-College Articulation of Alternative Educational Practices.* Eugene, Oreg.: author, December 1973.

Spurr, S. F. *Academic Degree Structures: Innovative Approaches.* New York: McGraw-Hill, 1970.

Tillery, D. *Distribution and Differentiation of Youth: A Study of Transition from School to College.* Cambridge, Mass.: Ballinger Publishing Co., 1973.

Credit by Examination

Casserly, P. L. *A Selected Bibliography of References on the Advanced Placement Program of the College Entrance Examination Board.* Princeton, N.J.: Educational Testing Service, 1974.

Casserly, P. L.; Peterson, R. E.; and Coffman, W. E. *College Decision on Advanced Placement Policies and Practices at Sixty-Three Colleges.* Princeton, N.J.: Educational Testing Service, 1965.

College Entrance Examination Board. *CLEP May Be for You.* New York: College Entrance Examination Board, 1973.

College Entrance Examination Board. *CLEP General and Subject Examinations: Descriptions and Sample Questions.* New York: College Entrance Examination Board, 1974.

College Entrance Examination Board. *College-Level Examination Program Description and Uses.* New York: College Entrance Examination Board, 1967.

Enger, J. M., and Whitney, D. R. "CLEP Credit and Graduation: A Four-Year Study of the University of Iowa." *College and University,* Spring 1974.

Haag, C. H. "Credit by Examination." In *Findings.* Princeton, N.J.: Educational Testing Service, 1975.

Howard, T. A. "Credit by Examination: Giving Credit Where Credit Is Due." *Future Talk.* September 1974. California State University and Colleges, Office of the Chancellor.

Kreplin, H. *Credit by Examination: A Review and Analysis of the Literature.* Berkeley, Calif.: Ford Foundation Program for Research in University Administration, Grant No. 680-026A, July 1971.

Historical Perspectives on High School-College Articulation

Chase, W. J., and Thurber, C. H. "Preliminary Report of the Committee on College Entrance Requirements." *School Review* 4 (1896): 341.

Eliot, C. "The Gray Between the Elementary Schools and the Colleges." *National Education Association Proceedings* 29 (1890): 523.

Fischer, H. A. "Uniform Requirements for Admissions." *National Education Association Proceedings* 29 (1890): 706.

Gerhard, D. "Emergence of the Credit System in American Education Considered as a Problem of Social and Intellectual History." *American Association of University Professors Bulletin* 41 (1955): 647-668.

Moore, F. W. "The Equalization of Requirements for Admissions into Different Courses Leading to the First Collegiate Degree." *School Review* 10 (1902): 217.

Traxler, A., and Townsend, A., eds. *Improving Transition from School to College.* New York: Harper and Brothers, 1953.

Inter-Institutional Credit Transfer

Dearing, G. B. "Substantive Issues in the Transfer Problem." In *College Transfer: Working Papers and Recommendations from the Arlie House Conference,* December 1973. Washington, D.C.: Association Transfer Group, 1974, pp. 50-71.

Furniss, W. T., and Martin, M. Y. "Toward Solving Transfer Problems." In *College Transfer: Working Papers and Recommendations from the Arlie House Conference,* December 1973. Washington, D.C.: Association Transfer Group, 1974, pp. 7-25.

Kuhns, E. "A Resolution to End Transfer Hurdles." Washington, D.C.: American Association of Community and Junior Colleges, 1973. Mimeographed.

Martorana, S. V. "Organizing Approaches to Facilitate Student Mobility in Post-Secondary Education." In *College Transfer: Working Papers and Recommendations from the Arlie House Conference*, December 1973. Washington, D.C.: Association Transfer Group, 1974, pp. 107-127.

Menacker, J. *From School to College: Articulation and Transfer.* Washington, D.C.: American Council on Education, 1975.

Thomas, L. M. "Award of Transfer Credit: Policies and Practices." *College and University*, Fall 1971, pp. 30-35.

Willingham, W. W. "Transfer Standards and the Public Interest." In *College Transfer: Working Papers and Recommendations from the Arlie House Conference*, December 1973. Washington, D.C.: Association Transfer Group, 1974, pp. 26-49.

Willingham, W. W. *The No. 2 Access Problem: Transfer to the Upper Division.* Washington, D.C.: American Association for Higher Education, July 1972.